新丝路"中文＋职业技能"系列教材编写委员会
（中文＋酒店管理）

总策划：马箭飞　谢永华

策　划：邵旭波　邵亦鹏　张海宁

顾　问：朱志平（北京师范大学）
　　　　林秀琴（首都师范大学）
　　　　宋继华（北京师范大学）

总主编：谢永华　杜曾慧

中级教材

语言类主编：易　华　专业类主编：谈　慧

语言类副主编：周　波　史其慧

专业类副主编：张　瑜　周立军　王桂花

项目组长：郭凤岚

项目副组长：付彦白

项目成员：郭　冰　武传霞　齐　琰　赫　栗　李金梅

新丝路"中文+职业技能"系列教材
New Silk Road "Chinese + Vocational Skills" Series

中文+酒店管理
Chinese + Hotel Management

中级 Intermediate

新丝路"中文+职业技能"系列教材编写委员会　编

© 2023 北京语言大学出版社，社图号 23204

图书在版编目（CIP）数据

中文＋酒店管理．中级／新丝路"中文＋职业技能"系列教材编写委员会编．-- 北京：北京语言大学出版社，2023.12

新丝路"中文＋职业技能"系列教材
ISBN 978-7-5619-6424-8

Ⅰ.①中… Ⅱ.①新… Ⅲ.①汉语－对外汉语教学－教材 ②饭店－商业企业管理－教材 Ⅳ.① H195.4 ② F719.2

中国国家版本馆 CIP 数据核字（2023）第 227734 号

中文＋酒店管理（中级）
ZHONGWEN + JIUDIAN GUANLI (ZHONGJI)

排版制作：	北京创艺涵文化发展有限公司
责任印制：	周 燚

出版发行：	北京语言大学出版社
社　　址：	北京市海淀区学院路 15 号，100083
网　　址：	www.blcup.com
电子信箱：	service@blcup.com
电　　话：	编 辑 部　8610-82303647/3592/3395
	国内发行　8610-82303650/3591/3648
	海外发行　8610-82303365/3080/3668
	北语书店　8610-82303653
	网购咨询　8610-82303908
印　　刷：	北京富资园科技发展有限公司

版　次：	2023 年 12 月第 1 版	印　次：	2023 年 12 月第 1 次印刷
开　本：	889 毫米 × 1194 毫米　1/16	印　张：	11
字　数：	207 千字		
定　价：	98.00 元		

PRINTED IN CHINA
凡有印装质量问题，本社负责调换。售后QQ号 1367565611，电话 010-82303590

编写说明

新丝路"中文＋职业技能"系列教材是把中文作为第二语言，结合专业和职业的专门用途、职业用途的中文教材，不是专业理论教材，不是一般意义的通用综合中文教材。本系列教材定位为职场生存中文教材、立体式技能型语言教材。教材研发的目标是既要满足学习者一般中文环境下的基本交际需求，又要满足学习者职业学习需求和职场工作需求。它和普通的国际中文教材的区别不在语法，而在词汇的专门化程度，在中文的用途、使用场合、应用范围。目前，专门用途、职业用途的中文教材在语言分类和研究成果上几近空白，本系列教材的成功研发开创了中文学习的新视野、新领域、新方向，将"中文＋职业技能＋X等级证书"真正融合，使学习者在学习中文的同时，也可通过实践掌握职业技能，从而获得 X 等级证书。

适用对象

本系列教材将适用对象定位为双零基础（零语言基础、零技能基础）的来华学习中文和先进技能的长期或者短期进修生，可满足初、中、高各层次专业课程的教学需要。教材亦可供海内外相关的培训课程及"走出去"的中资企业培训本土化员工使用。

结构规模

本系列教材采取专项语言技能与职业技能训练相结合的中文教学及教材编写模式。教材选择当前热门的物流管理、汽车服务工程技术、电子商务、机电一体化、计算机网络技术、酒店管理等六个专业，培养各专业急需急用的技术岗位人才。每个专业教材均包括初、中、高级三册。每一册都配有专业视频教学资源，还附有"视频脚本""参考答案"等配套资源。

编写理念

本系列教材将词语进行分类，区分普通词语和专业词语，以通用语料为基础，以概念性、行为性词语为主，不脱离职场情境讨论分级，做到控制词汇量，控制工作场景，控制交流内容与方式，构建语义框架。将语言的分级和专业的分级科学地融合，是实现本系列教材成功编写的关键。

教材目标

语言技能目标：

初级阶段，能熟练掌握基础通用词语和职场的常用专业词语，能使用简短句子进行简单的生活及工作交流。中级阶段，能听懂工作场合简单的交谈与发言，明白大意，把握基本情况，能就工作中重要的话题用简单的话与人沟通。高级阶段，能听懂工作场合一般的交谈与发言，抓住主要内容和关键信息，使用基本交际策略与人交流、开展工作，能初步了解与交际活动相关的文化因素，掌握与交际有关的一般文化背景知识，能排除交际时遇到的文化障碍。交际能力层次的递进实现从初级的常规礼节、基本生活及工作的交流能力，到中级的简单的服务流程信息交流能力，最后达到高级的复杂信息的交流和特情处理的能力。

职业技能目标：

以满足岗位需求为目标，将遴选出的当前热门的专业工作岗位分为初、中、高三级。物流管理专业初、中、高级对应的岗位分别是物流员、物流经理、物流总监；汽车服务工程技术专业初、中、高级对应的岗位分别是汽车机电维修工、汽车服务顾问、技术总监；电子商务专业初、中、高级对应的岗位分别是电子商务运营助理、电子商务运营员、电子商务客服；机电一体化专业初、中、高级对应的岗位分别是机电操作工、机电调整工、机电维修工；计算机网络技术专业初、中、高级对应的岗位分别是宽带运维工程师、网络运维专员、网络管理员；酒店管理专业初、中、高级对应的岗位分别是前厅基层接待员、前厅主管、前厅经理。每个专业分解出三十个工作场景/任务，学习者在学习后能够全面掌握此岗位的概况及基本程序，实现语言学习和专业操作的双重目标。

编写原则

1. 语言知识技能与专业知识技能并进，满足当前热门的、急需急用的岗位需求。

2. 渐进分化，综合贯通，拆解难点，分而治之。

3. 语言知识与专业知识科学、高效复现，语言技能与专业技能螺旋式上升，职场情境、语义框架、本体输入方式相互配合。

4. 使用大量的图片和视频，实现专业知识和技能呈现形式可视化。

5. 强化专业岗位实操性技能。本系列教材配有专业技术教学的视频，突出展示专业岗位的实操性技能，语言学习难度与技能掌握难度的不匹配可通过实操性强的视频和实训环节来补充。

特色追求

本系列教材从初级最基础的语音知识学习和岗位认知开始，将"中文+职业技能"融入在工作场景对话中，把工作分解成一个个任务，用图片认知的方式解决专业词语的认知问题，用视频展示的方法解决学习者掌握中文词语与专业技能的不匹配问题，注重技能的实操性，注重"在做中学"。每一单元都设置了"学以致用"板块，目的不仅仅是解决本单元任务的词语认知问题，更是将学习的目标放在"能听""能用""能模仿说出"上。我们力争通过大量图片的使用和配套视频的展示，将教材打造成立体式、技能型语言教材，方便学习者能够更好地自主学习。

使用建议

1. 本系列教材每个专业分为初、中、高级三册，每册10单元，初级每单元建议8～10课时完成，中级10～12课时完成，高级12～14课时完成。

2. 教材注释和说明着力于简明扼要，注重实操性，注重听说技能培养，对于教材涉及的语法知识，教师可视情况予以细化和补充。

3. "单元实训"板块可以在课文和语言点学完之后作为课堂练习使用，建议2课时完成。教师要带着学习者按照实训步骤一步步完成，实训步骤不要求学习者能够看懂、读懂，重要的是教师要引领操作，实现学习者掌握专业技能的目标。

4. "单元小结"板块是对整个单元关键词语和核心内容的总结，对于这部分内容，教师要进行听说练习，以便更好地帮助学习者了解本单元的核心工作任务。

5. 教师上课时要充分利用教材设计的练习，引导学习者多听多练，听说结合，学做合一。

6. 教师要带着学习者熟练诵读课文，要求学习者把每课的关键词语和句子、课堂用语背诵下来。

特别感谢

感谢教育部中外语言交流合作中心将新丝路"中文＋职业技能"系列教材列为重点研发项目，为我们教材编写增添了动力和责任感。教材编写委员会负责整套教材的规划、设计与编写协调，并先后召开上百次讨论会，对每册教材的课文编写、体例安排、注释说明、练习设计、图片选择、视频制作等进行全方位的评估、讨论和审定。感谢编写委员会成员和所有编者高度的敬业精神、精益求精的编写态度，以及所投入的热情和精力、付出的心血与智慧。感谢关注本系列教材并贡献宝贵意见的国际中文教育教学界专家和全国各地的同人。

新丝路"中文＋职业技能"系列教材编写委员会

2023年4月

Compilation Instructions

The New Silk Road "Chinese + Vocational Skills" is a series of Chinese textbooks for specialized and vocational purposes that combine professional and vocational technologies with Chinese as a second language. Instead of being specialized theoretical textbooks, or comprehensive or universal Chinese textbooks in a general sense, this series is intended to be Chinese textbooks for career survival, and three-dimensional skills-based language textbooks. The textbooks are developed with a view to meeting students' basic communication needs in general Chinese environment, and their professional learning needs and workplace demands as well. They are different from ordinary Chinese textbooks for foreigners in the degree of specialization of vocabulary, in the purpose, usage occasion, and application scope of Chinese (not in grammar). At present, Chinese textbooks for specialized and vocational purposes are virtually non-existent in terms of language classification and research results, so the successful development of this series has opened up new horizons, new fields and new directions for Chinese learning, and virtually integrated "Chinese + Vocational Skills + X-Level Certificates", which enables students to practically master vocational skills and obtain X-level certificates while learning Chinese.

Applicable Targets

This series is targeted at long-term or short-term students who come to China to learn Chinese and advanced skills with zero language basis and zero skill basis, which can meet the teaching needs of the elementary, intermediate and advanced specialized courses. This series can also be used for relevant training courses at home and abroad and for Chinese-funded enterprises that "go global" to train local employees.

Structure and Scale

This series adopts a Chinese teaching and textbook compilation model combining special language skills and vocational skills training. The series includes the textbooks for six popular majors such as logistics management, automotive service engineering technology, e-commerce, mechatronics, computer networking technology, and hotel management to cultivate technical talents in urgent need. The textbooks for each major consist of the textbooks at the elementary, intermediate and advanced levels. Each textbook is equipped with professional video teaching resources, and "video scripts", "reference answers" and other supporting resources as well.

Compilation Concept

This series classifies the vocabulary into general vocabulary and specialized vocabulary. Based on the general vocabulary, it focuses on conceptual and behavioral words, not deviating from workplace situations, so as to control the vocabulary, work scenarios and content and means of communication, and build the semantic framework. The scientific integration of language classification and specialty classification is the key to the successful compilation of textbooks.

Textbook Objectives

Language Skill Objectives

For students at the elementary level, they are trained to be familiar with basic general vocabulary and common specialized vocabulary in the workplace, and be able to use short sentences for simple communication in life and at work. For those at the intermediate level, they are trained to understand simple conversations and speeches in the workplace, comprehend the main ideas, grasp the basic situations, and communicate with others in simple words on important topics at work. For those at the advanced level, they are trained to be able to understand general conversations and speeches in the workplace, grasp the main content and key information, use basic communication strategies to communicate with others and carry out the work, have a preliminary understanding of cultural factors related to communication activities, master the general communication-related cultural background knowledge, and overcome cultural barriers encountered during communication. The progression in level of communicative competence helps them to leap forward from routine etiquette, basic communication in life and at work at the elementary level, to simple information exchange of service processes at the intermediate level, and finally to complex information exchange and handling of special circumstances at the advanced level.

Vocational Skill Objectives

To meet job requirements at the elementary, intermediate and advanced levels, the professional positions that are most urgently needed overseas are selected. The positions corresponding to logistics management at the elementary, intermediate and advanced levels are logistics staff, logistics managers and logistics directors; the positions corresponding to automotive service engineering technology at the elementary, intermediate and advanced levels are automotive electromechanical maintenance staff, automotive service consultants and technical directors; the positions corresponding to e-commerce at the elementary, intermediate and advanced levels are electronic operation assistants, e-commerce operators and e-commerce customer service staff; the positions corresponding to mechatronics at the elementary, intermediate and advanced levels are mechanical and electrical operators, mechanical and electrical adjusters, and mechanical and electrical maintenance staff; the positions corresponding to computer networking techology at the elementary, intermediate and advanced levels are broadband operation and maintenance engineers, network operation and maintenance specialists, and network administrators; the positions corresponding to hotel management at the elementary, intermediate and advanced levels are lobby receptionists, lobby supervisors and lobby managers. Through 30 work scenarios/tasks set for each major, learners can fully grasp the general situations and basic procedures of the position after learning, and achieve the dual goals of language learning and professional operation.

Principles of Compilation

1. Language knowledge skills and professional knowledge skills go hand in hand to meet the demands of current popular and urgently needed job positions;

2. It makes progressive differentiation and comprehensive integration, breaking down, dividing and conquering difficult points;

3. Language knowledge and professional knowledge recur scientifically and efficiently, language skills and professional skills spiral upward, and the situational stage, semantic framework, and ontology input methods cooperate with each other;

4. Professional knowledge and skills are visualized, using a lot of pictures and videos;

5. It strengthens the practical skills in professional positions. This series of textbooks is equipped with videos of professional technical training, highlighting the practical skills for professional positions. It addresses the mismatch between the difficulty of language learning and that of mastering skills by supplementing with practical videos and practical training.

Characteristic Pursuit

Starting from the basic phonetic knowledge learning and job cognition at the elementary level, this series integrates "Chinese + Vocational Skills" into the working scene dialogues, breaking down the job into various tasks, solving lexical students' problems by means of picture cognition, solving the problem of the mismatch between students' mastery of Chinese vocabulary and professional skills by means of displaying videos, stressing the practicality of skills, and focusing on "learning by doing". Each unit has a "Practicing What You Have Learnt" module, which not only solves the problem of lexical cognition of this unit, but also takes "being able to comprehend", "being able to use" and "being able to imitate" as the learning objectives. We strive to use a large number of pictures and display supporting videos to build the textbooks into three-dimensional skills-based language teaching materials, so that learners can learn more independently.

Recommendations for Use

1. Each major of this series consists of three volumes at the elementary, intermediate, and advanced levels, with 10 units in each volume. For each unit, it is recommended to be completed in 8-10 class hours at the elementary level, 10-12 class hours at the intermediate level, and 12-14 class hours at the advanced level.

2. The notes and explanations in the textbooks focus on conciseness, practicality, and the training of listening and speaking skills. The grammar knowledge in the textbooks can be detailed and supplemented by teachers as the case may be.

3. "Unit Practical Training" module can be used as a classroom exercise after the texts and language points, preferably to be completed in two class hours. Teachers should guide students to complete the training tasks step by step. Students are not required to read and understand the training steps. It is important that teachers guide students to achieve the goal of mastering professional skills.

4. "Unit Summary" module summarizes the keywords and core content of the entire unit. Through listening and speaking exercises, this part can better help learners understand the core tasks of this unit.

5. Teachers should make full use of the exercises designed in the textbooks during class, and guide students to listen more and practice more, combine listening and speaking, and integrate learning with practice.

6. Teachers should guide students to proficiently read the texts aloud, asking them to recite the keywords, sentences and classroom expressions in each unit.

Acknowledgements

We are grateful to the Center for Language Education and Cooperation of the Ministry of Education for listing the New Silk Road "Chinese + Vocational Skills" series as a key research and development project, which adds motivation and a sense of responsibility to our textbook compilation. The Textbook Compilation Committee is responsible for the planning, design, compilation and coordination of the entire set of textbooks, and has held hundreds of seminars to conduct a comprehensive evaluation, discussion, examination and approval of text compilation, style arrangement, notes and explanations, exercise design, picture selection, and video production of each textbook. We are indebted to the members of the Compilation Committee and all compilers for their professional dedication, unwavering pursuit of perfection in the compilation, as well as their enthusiasm, hard work and wisdom. We are thankful to the experts in international Chinese language education and colleagues from all over the country who have kept a close eye on this series and contributed their valuable opinions.

Compilation Committee of New Silk Road "Chinese + Vocational Skills" Series

April 2023

gǎngwèi jièshào
岗位介绍
Posts Introduction

qiántīngbù jīnglǐ
前厅部经理
Front Office Manager

qiántái jiēdàiyuán
前台接待员
Receptionist

zǒngjī jiēxiànyuán
总机接线员
Telephone Operator

lǐbīnyuán
礼宾员
Concierge

dàtáng jīnglǐ
大堂经理
Lobby Manager

qiántái zhǔguǎn
前台主管
Reception Supervisor

语法术语及缩略形式参照表
Abbreviations of Grammar Terms

Grammar Terms in Chinese	Grammar Terms in Pinyin	Grammar Terms in English	Abbreviations
名词	míngcí	noun	n.
专有名词	zhuānyǒu míngcí	proper noun	pn.
代词	dàicí	pronoun	pron.
数词	shùcí	numeral	num.
量词	liàngcí	measure word	m.
数量词	shùliàngcí	quantifier	q.
动词	dòngcí	verb	v.
助动词	zhùdòngcí	auxiliary	aux.
形容词	xíngróngcí	adjective	adj.
副词	fùcí	adverb	adv.
介词	jiècí	preposition	prep.
连词	liáncí	conjunction	conj.
助词	zhùcí	particle	part.
拟声词	nǐshēngcí	onomatopoeia	onom.
叹词	tàncí	interjection	int.
前缀	qiánzhuì	prefix	pref.
后缀	hòuzhuì	suffix	suf.
成语	chéngyǔ	idiom	idm.
短语	duǎnyǔ	phrase	phr.
主语	zhǔyǔ	subject	S
谓语	wèiyǔ	predicate	P
宾语	bīnyǔ	object	O
定语	dìngyǔ	attributive	Attrib
状语	zhuàngyǔ	adverbial	Adverb
补语	bǔyǔ	complement	C

CONTENTS 目 录

第一单元　酒店设施　Unit 1　Hotel Facilities		1
第一部分　课文　**Texts**		2
一、热身 Warm-up		2
二、课文 Texts		3
三、视听说 Viewing, Listening and Speaking		6
四、学以致用 Practicing What You Have Learnt		7
五、小知识 Tips		8
第二部分　汉字　**Chinese Characters**		9
一、汉字知识 Knowledge about Chinese Characters		9
1. 汉字的笔画（1） Strokes of Chinese characters (1)		
一 丨 丿 丶		
2. 汉字的笔顺（1） Stroke orders of Chinese characters (1)		
先横后竖 Horizontal strokes before vertical strokes		
先撇后捺 Left-falling strokes before right-falling strokes		
二、汉字认读与书写 The Recognition and Writing of Chinese Characters		9
第三部分　日常用语　**Daily Expressions**		10
第四部分　单元实训　**Unit Practical Training**		10
模拟介绍酒店设施 Simulated Introduction to Hotel Facilities		10
第五部分　单元小结　**Unit Summary**		11
第二单元　团队入住登记　Unit 2　Group Check-in		13
第一部分　课文　**Texts**		14
一、热身 Warm-up		14
二、课文 Texts		16
三、视听说 Viewing, Listening and Speaking		21
四、学以致用 Practicing What You Have Learnt		22
五、小知识 Tips		24
第二部分　汉字　**Chinese Characters**		25
一、汉字知识 Knowledge about Chinese Characters		25

I

1. 汉字的笔画（2） Strokes of Chinese characters (2)
　　丶 フ ㄟ ㇏

2. 汉字的笔顺（2） Stroke orders of Chinese characters (2)
　　先上后下 Upper strokes before lower strokes
　　先左后右 Left-side strokes before right-side strokes

　　二、汉字认读与书写 The Recognition and Writing of Chinese Characters　　25

第三部分　日常用语　**Daily Expressions**　　26

第四部分　单元实训　**Unit Practical Training**　　26
　　模拟办理团体入住 Simulated Group Check-in　　26

第五部分　单元小结　**Unit Summary**　　27

第三单元　调换房间　Unit 3　Changing into Another Room　　29

第一部分　课文　**Texts**　　30
　　一、热身 Warm-up　　30
　　二、课文 Texts　　31
　　三、视听说 Viewing, Listening and Speaking　　34
　　四、学以致用 Practicing What You Have Learnt　　35
　　五、小知识 Tips　　36

第二部分　汉字　**Chinese Characters**　　37
　　一、汉字知识 Knowledge about Chinese Characters　　37

1. 汉字的笔画（3） Strokes of Chinese characters (3)
　　㇆ 亅 ㇉ ㇄

2. 汉字的笔顺（3） Stroke orders of Chinese characters (3)
　　先中间后两边 Strokes in the middle before those on both sides
　　先外边后里边 Outside strokes before inside strokes

　　二、汉字认读与书写 The Recognition and Writing of Chinese Characters　　37

第三部分　日常用语　**Daily Expressions**　　38

第四部分　单元实训　**Unit Practical Training**　　38
　　模拟调换房间 Simulated Room into Another Changing　　38

第五部分　单元小结　**Unit Summary**　　39

第四单元　续住服务　Unit 4　Extended-Stay Service　　41

第一部分　课文　**Texts**　　42
　　一、热身 Warm-up　　42
　　二、课文 Texts　　43

三、视听说 Viewing, Listening and Speaking		46
四、学以致用 Practicing What You Have Learnt		48
五、小知识 Tips		49

第二部分 汉字　**Chinese Characters**　49
　　一、汉字知识 Knowledge about Chinese Characters　49
　　　　1. 汉字的笔画（4）　Strokes of Chinese characters (4)
　　　　2. 汉字的笔顺（4）　Stroke orders of Chinese characters (4)
　　　　　先外后里再封口 Outside strokes before inside strokes, and then sealing strokes
　　二、汉字认读与书写 The Recognition and Writing of Chinese Characters　50

第三部分 日常用语　**Daily Expressions**　50

第四部分 单元实训　**Unit Practical Training**　50
　　模拟续住服务 Simulated Extended-Stay Service　50

第五部分 单元小结　**Unit Summary**　51

第五单元　行李服务　Unit 5　Luggage Service　53

第一部分 课文　**Texts**　54
　　一、热身 Warm-up　54
　　二、课文 Texts　55
　　三、视听说 Viewing, Listening and Speaking　58
　　四、学以致用 Practicing What You Have Learnt　60
　　五、小知识 Tips　60

第二部分 汉字　**Chinese Characters**　61
　　一、汉字知识 Knowledge about Chinese Characters　61
　　　　1. 汉字的笔画（5）　Strokes of Chinese characters (5)
　　　　2. 汉字的结构（1）　Structures of Chinese characters (1)
　　　　　独体结构 Independent structure
　　二、汉字认读与书写 The Recognition and Writing of Chinese Characters　62

第三部分 日常用语　**Daily Expressions**　62

第四部分 单元实训　**Unit Practical Training**　62
　　模拟行李服务 Simulated Luggage Service　62

第五部分 单元小结　**Unit Summary**　63

III

第六单元　网络服务　Unit 6　Internet Service　65

第一部分　课文　Texts　66
- 一、热身 Warm-up　66
- 二、课文 Texts　67
- 三、视听说 Viewing, Listening and Speaking　71
- 四、学以致用 Practicing What You Have Learnt　73
- 五、小知识 Tips　73

第二部分　汉字　Chinese Characters　74
- 一、汉字知识 Knowledge about Chinese Characters　74
  1. 汉字的笔画（6）　Strokes of Chinese characters (6)
     乛 乛
  2. 汉字的结构（2）　Structures of Chinese characters (2)
     品字形结构　品-shaped structure
- 二、汉字认读与书写 The Recognition and Writing of Chinese Characters　74

第三部分　日常用语　Daily Expressions　75

第四部分　单元实训　Unit Practical Training　75
模拟酒店无线网络服务 Simulated Hotel Wi-Fi Service　75

第五部分　单元小结　Unit Summary　76

第七单元　房内用餐服务　Unit 7　In-room Dining Service　79

第一部分　课文　Texts　80
- 一、热身 Warm-up　80
- 二、课文 Texts　81
- 三、视听说 Viewing, Listening and Speaking　85
- 四、学以致用 Practicing What You Have Learnt　86
- 五、小知识 Tips　86

第二部分　汉字　Chinese Characters　87
- 一、汉字知识 Knowledge about Chinese Characters　87
  1. 汉字的笔画（7）　Strokes of Chinese characters (7)
     𠃌 乁
  2. 汉字的结构（3）　Structures of Chinese characters (3)
     上下结构 Top-bottom structure
     上中下结构 Top-middle-bottom structure
- 二、汉字认读与书写 The Recognition and Writing of Chinese Characters　88

第三部分　日常用语　Daily Expressions　88

IV

第四部分　单元实训　Unit Practical Training　　　　　　　　　　　　　88
　　　模拟房内用餐服务 Simulated In-room Dining Service　　　　　　　88

第五部分　单元小结　Unit Summary　　　　　　　　　　　　　　　89

第八单元　租借物品服务　Unit 8　Rental Service　　　91

第一部分　课文　Texts　　　　　　　　　　　　　　　　　　　92
　　一、热身 Warm-up　　　　　　　　　　　　　　　　　　92
　　二、课文 Texts　　　　　　　　　　　　　　　　　　　93
　　三、视听说 Viewing, Listening and Speaking　　　　　　　96
　　四、学以致用 Practicing What You Have Learnt　　　　　　97
　　五、小知识 Tips　　　　　　　　　　　　　　　　　　　98

第二部分　汉字　Chinese Characters　　　　　　　　　　　　　99
　　一、汉字知识 Knowledge about Chinese Characters　　　　　99
　　　1. 汉字的笔画（8） Strokes of Chinese characters (8)
　　　　乚 乙
　　　2. 汉字的结构（4） Structures of Chinese characters (4)
　　　　左右结构 Left-right structure
　　　　左中右结构 Left-middle-right structure
　　二、汉字认读与书写 The Recognition and Writing of Chinese Characters　　99

第三部分　日常用语　Daily Expressions　　　　　　　　　　　　99

第四部分　单元实训　Unit Practical Training　　　　　　　　　100
　　　模拟酒店租借物品服务 Simulated Rental Service in a Hotel　　100

第五部分　单元小结　Unit Summary　　　　　　　　　　　　　100

第九单元　城市及旅游信息服务　Unit 9　City and Tourism Information Service　103

第一部分　课文　Texts　　　　　　　　　　　　　　　　　　104
　　一、热身 Warm-up　　　　　　　　　　　　　　　　　104
　　二、课文 Texts　　　　　　　　　　　　　　　　　　　105
　　三、视听说 Viewing, Listening and Speaking　　　　　　　110
　　四、学以致用 Practicing What You Have Learnt　　　　　111
　　五、小知识 Tips　　　　　　　　　　　　　　　　　　112

第二部分　汉字　Chinese Characters　　　　　　　　　　　　112
　　一、汉字知识 Knowledge about Chinese Characters　　　　112
　　　1. 汉字的笔画（9） Strokes of Chinese characters (9)
　　　　乛 乚

2. 汉字的结构（5） Structures of Chinese characters (5)
   全包围结构 Fully-enclosed structure
   半包围结构 Semi-enclosed structure

　　　　二、汉字认读与书写 The Recognition and Writing of Chinese Characters　　113

第三部分　日常用语　**Daily Expressions**　　113

第四部分　单元实训　**Unit Practical Training**　　114

　　模拟城市及旅游信息服务 Simulated City and Tourism Information Service　　114

第五部分　单元小结　**Unit Summary**　　114

第十单元　团队退房服务　Unit 10　Group Check-out Service　　117

第一部分　课文　**Texts**　　118
　　一、热身 Warm-up　　118
　　二、课文 Texts　　119
　　三、视听说 Viewing, Listening and Speaking　　123
　　四、学以致用 Practicing What You Have Learnt　　124
　　五、小知识 Tips　　125

第二部分　汉字　**Chinese Characters**　　126
　　一、汉字知识 Knowledge about Chinese Characters　　126
　　　　1. 汉字的笔画（总表） Strokes of Chinese characters (general table)
　　　　2. 汉字的笔顺（总表） Stroke orders of Chinese characters (general table)
　　　　3. 汉字的结构（总表） Structures of Chinese characters(general table)
　　二、汉字认读与书写 The Recognition and Writing of Chinese Characters　　127

第三部分　日常用语　**Daily Expressions**　　127

第四部分　单元实训　**Unit Practical Training**　　127

　　模拟酒店团队退房服务 Simulated Group Check-out Service in a Hotel　　127

第五部分　单元小结　**Unit Summary**　　128

附录　Appendixes　　130

词汇总表　**Vocabulary**　　130
日常用语　**Daily Expressions**　　139
视频脚本　**Video Scripts**　　142
参考答案　**Reference Answers**　　154

1

Jiǔdiàn shèshī
酒店设施
Hotel Facilities

jiǔdiàn jīběn shèshī
酒店基本设施
Basic Hotel Facilities

zhōngcāntīng
中餐厅
Chinese restaurant

xīcāntīng
西餐厅
Western restaurant

dàtángbā
大堂吧
Lobby bar

huìyìshì
会议室
Conference room

yóuyǒngchí
游泳池
Swimming pool

题解 Introduction

1. 学习内容：酒店基本设施的名称和功能。
   Learning content: The names and functions of basic hotel facilities.
2. 知识目标：掌握酒店基本设施相关的核心词语，学习汉字的笔画"一""丨""丿""乀"、笔顺"先横后竖、先撇后捺"，学写本单元相关汉字。
   Knowledge objectives: To master the core vocabulary related to basic hotel facilities, learn the strokes "一", "丨", "丿", "乀" and the stroke orders "horizontal strokes before vertical strokes", "left-falling strokes before right-falling strokes" of Chinese characters, and write the characters related to this unit.
3. 技能目标：能正确应对客人对酒店设施方面的询问。
   Skill objective: To be able to make proper response to a guest's inquiries about hotel facilities.

第一部分 Part 1

课文 Texts

一、热身 rèshēn Warm-up

1. 给词语选择对应的图片。 **Choose the corresponding pictures for the words.**

A

B

C

D

① cāntīng
餐厅_____
dining room

② jiànshēnfáng
健身房_____
gym

③ huìyìshì
会议室_____
conference room

④ yóuyǒngchí
游泳池_____
swimming pool

酒店设施 1
Hotel Facilities

2. 观看介绍酒店设施的视频，并选择正确的营业时间。
Watch the video about hotel facilities and choose the right opening hours.

    wǎnshang 8 diǎn dào 12 diǎn
A. 晚上 8 点到 12 点
    from 8 to 12 p.m.

    zhōngwǔ 11 diǎn dào xiàwǔ 2 diǎn
B. 中午 11 点到 下午 2 点
    from 11 a.m. to 2 p.m.

    zǎoshang 8 diǎn dào wǎnshang 9 diǎn
C. 早上 8 点到 晚上 9 点
    from 8 a.m. to 9 p.m.

    zǎoshang 7 diǎn dào zhōngwǔ 11 diǎn
D. 早上 7 点到 中午 11 点
    from 7 a.m. to 11 a.m.

zhōngcāntīng
❶ 中餐厅 _____
Chinese restaurant

dàtángbā
❷ 大堂吧_____
lobby bar

xīcāntīng
❸ 西餐厅_____
Western restaurant

huìyìshì
❹ 会议室_____
conference room

二、课文　kèwén　Texts

A 🎧 01-01

kèrén: Dǎrǎo yíxià, cāntīng zài nǎlǐ?
客人：打扰一下，餐厅 在哪里？

qiántái jiēdàiyuán: Nín hǎo, wǒmen yǒu yí gè zhōngcāntīng hé yí gè xīcāntīng, nín xǐhuan nǎ
前台 接待员：您 好，我们 有一个 中餐厅 和一个西餐厅，您喜欢哪
　　　　　　yí gè?
　　　　　　一个？

kèrén: Wǒ xiǎng chángchang zhōngcāntīng de shíwù.
客人：我 想 尝尝 中餐厅 的 食物。

qiántái jiēdàiyuán: Zhōngcāntīng zài èr lóu.
前台 接待员：中餐厅 在二楼。

3

kèrén:		Cāntīng shénme shíjiān yíngyè?
客人:		餐厅什么时间营业？
qiántái jiēdàiyuán:		Zǎocān cóng zǎoshang 6 diǎn dào 10 diǎn, wǔcān cóng zhōngwǔ 11 diǎn bàn
前台 接待员:		早餐从早上6点到10点，午餐从中午11点半
		dào xiàwǔ 2 diǎn, wǎncān cóng xiàwǔ 6 diǎn kāishǐ, 9 diǎn bàn jiéshù.
		到下午2点，晚餐从下午6点开始，9点半结束。
kèrén:		Hǎo de, xièxie. Xiànzài jǐ diǎn?
客人:		好的，谢谢。现在几点？
qiántái jiēdàiyuán:		Xiànzài shì xiàwǔ 6 diǎn bàn.
前台 接待员:		现在是下午6点半。
kèrén:		Nà wǒ kěyǐ qù cāntīng yòngcān le.
客人:		那我可以去餐厅用餐了。
qiántái jiēdàiyuán:		Shìde, zhù nín yòngcān yúkuài!
前台 接待员:		是的，祝您用餐愉快！

译文 yìwén Text in English

Guest: Excuse me, where is the restaurant?

Receptionist: Hello, we have a Chinese restaurant and a Western restaurant. Which one do you prefer?

Guest: I'd like to try some Chinese food.

Receptionist: The Chinese restaurant is on the second floor.

Guest: When is the restaurant open?

Receptionist: Breakfast is served from 6:00 a.m. to 10:00 a.m., lunch is served from 11:30 a.m. to 2:00 p.m., and supper is served from 6:00 p.m. to 9:30 p.m.

Guest: OK, thank you. What time is it?

Receptionist: It's 6:30 p.m.

Guest: Then I can go to the restaurant for dinner.

Receptionist: Yes, enjoy your meal!

普通词语 pǔtōng cíyǔ General Vocabulary 🎧 01-02

1.	喜欢	xǐhuan	v.	like
2.	尝	cháng	v.	try, taste
3.	食物	shíwù	n.	food
4.	楼	lóu	n.	floor
5.	午餐	wǔcān	n.	lunch
6.	晚餐	wǎncān	n.	supper

酒店设施
Hotel Facilities 1

专业词语 zhuānyè cíyǔ Specialized Vocabulary 🎧 01-03

1.	中餐厅	zhōngcāntīng	phr.	Chinese restaurant
2.	西餐厅	xīcāntīng	phr.	Western restaurant
3.	营业	yíngyè	v.	be open

B 🎧 01-04

前台 接待员 qiántái jiēdàiyuán: 您好，请问有什么可以帮到您？
Nín hǎo, qǐngwèn yǒu shénme kěyǐ bāngdào nín?

客人 kèrén: 您好，请问会议室在哪里？
Nín hǎo, qǐngwèn huìyìshì zài nǎlǐ?

前台 接待员 qiántái jiēdàiyuán: 会议室在三楼。
Huìyìshì zài sān lóu.

客人 kèrén: 好的，请问健身房在哪里？
Hǎo de, qǐngwèn jiànshēnfáng zài nǎlǐ?

前台 接待员 qiántái jiēdàiyuán: 健身房在五楼。
Jiànshēnfáng zài wǔ lóu.

客人 kèrén: 可以游泳吗？
Kěyǐ yóuyǒng ma?

前台 接待员 qiántái jiēdàiyuán: 酒店的游泳池在四楼。
Jiǔdiàn de yóuyǒngchí zài sì lóu.

客人 kèrén: 请问晚餐几点结束？
Qǐngwèn wǎncān jǐ diǎn jiéshù?

前台 接待员 qiántái jiēdàiyuán: 西餐厅营业到晚上10点，中餐厅营业到晚上9点。
Xīcāntīng yíngyè dào wǎnshang 10 diǎn, zhōngcāntīng yíngyè dào wǎnshang 9 diǎn.

客人 kèrén: 好的，谢谢。
Hǎo de, xièxie.

译文 yìwén Text in English

Receptionist: Hello, may I help you?

Guest: Hello, could you tell me where the conference room is?

Receptionist: It's on the third floor.

Guest: OK. Where is the gym, please?

Receptionist: It's on the fifth floor.

Guest: Can I swim?

Receptionist: The hotel's swimming pool is on the fourth floor.

Guest: May I ask what time supper ends?

Receptionist: The Western restaurant is open until 10 p.m., and the Chinese restaurant is open until 9 p.m.
Guest: OK, thank you.

普通词语 pǔtōng cíyǔ General Vocabulary 🎧 01-05

| 游泳 | yóuyǒng | v./n. | swim |

专业词语 zhuānyè cíyǔ Specialized Vocabulary 🎧 01-06

1.	会议室	huìyìshì	n.	conference room
2.	游泳池	yóuyǒngchí	n.	swimming pool
3.	健身房	jiànshēnfáng	n.	gym

三、视听说 shì-tīng-shuō Viewing, Listening and Speaking

1. 观看前台接待员帮旅行团领队办理团体客人入住登记的视频，根据听到的内容选择正确选项，并说出酒店的各种设施及营业时间。

Watch the video about the receptionist helping the tour leader check in group guests. Choose the right answers based on what you hear, and tell the facilities and opening hours of the hotel.

qiántái jiēdàiyuán: Nín hǎo, zhè shì nín kèrénmen de fángkǎ.
前台 接待员：您好，这是您客人们的房卡。

lǚxíngtuán lǐngduì: Hǎo de, xièxie.
旅行团 领队：好的，谢谢。

qiántái jiēdàiyuán: Rùzhù qián wǒ xiàng nín jièshào yíxià ❶ yǐjí ❷。
前台 接待员：入住前我向您介绍一下 ❶ 以及 ❷ 。

lǚxíngtuán lǐngduì: Hǎo de.
旅行团 领队：好的。

qiántái jiēdàiyuán: Zǎocān cāntīng zài jiǔdiàn de yī lóu, zǎocān shíjiān wéi zǎoshang 8 diǎn dào 10 diǎn. Jiǔdiàn
前台 接待员：早餐餐厅在酒店的一楼，早餐时间为早上 8 点到 10 点。酒店
huìyìshì zài èr lóu, jiànshēnfáng zài sān lóu.
会议室在二楼，健身房 在 三 楼。

lǚxíngtuán lǐngduì: Hǎo de, qǐngwèn jiǔdiàn yǒu xīcāntīng ma?
旅行团 领队：好的，请问 酒店有西餐厅吗？

酒店设施 1
Hotel Facilities

qiántái jiēdàiyuán: Yǒu de, xīcāntīng zài dǐnglóu, kěyǐ kàndào
前台 接待员： 有的，西餐厅在顶楼，可以看到 ③ 。

lǚxíngtuán lǐngduì: Hǎo de, xièxie. Qiántái néng ma?
旅行团 领队： 好的，谢谢。前台能 ④ 吗？

qiántái jiēdàiyuán: Nín kěyǐ shǐyòng fángjiān nèi tígōng de
前台 接待员： 您可以使用 房间内提供的 ⑤ 。

lǚxíngtuán lǐngduì: Hǎo de, zhīdào le, xièxie.
旅行团 领队： 好的，知道了，谢谢。

qiántái jiēdàiyuán: Bú kèqi, zhù nín rùzhù yúkuài!
前台 接待员： 不客气，祝您入住愉快！

bǎoxiǎnxiāng
A. 保险箱
safe box

chéngshì jǐngguān
B. 城市 景观
urban landscape

yíngyè shíjiān
C. 营业时间
opening hours

bǎoguǎn guìzhòng wùpǐn
D. 保管 贵重 物品
keep the valuables

jiǔdiàn de shèshī
E. 酒店的设施
hotel facilities

2. 说一说　Let's talk.

练习说一说酒店的各种设施类型。　Talk about various hotel facilities.

四、学以致用　xuéyǐzhìyòng　Practicing What You Have Learnt

观看客人询问前台接待员关于酒店洗衣房信息的对话视频，对下列服务用语进行排序。
Watch the video about the guest inquiring the receptionist about the hotel laundry. Arrange the following service expressions in order.

Xǐyīfáng shì miǎnfèi shǐyòng de ma?
❶ 洗衣房是免费使用的吗？
Is the laundry free to use?

Fēicháng gǎnxiè.
② 非常感谢。
Thank you very much.

Qǐngwèn jiǔdiàn xǐyīfáng zài nǎlǐ?
③ 请问酒店洗衣房在哪里？
Excuse me, where is the hotel laundry?

Shìde, xǐyīfáng shì miǎnfèi shǐyòng de.
④ 是的，洗衣房是免费使用的。
Yes, it is used for free.

Bú kèqi!
⑤ 不客气！
You're welcome!

Jiǔdiàn xǐyīfáng zài wǔ lóu.
⑥ 酒店洗衣房在五楼。
The hotel laundry is on the fifth floor.

五、小知识　xiǎo zhīshi　Tips

Chuántǒng de jiǔdiàn fēnlèifǎ shì gēnjù bùtóng de shìchǎng dìngwèi hé kèyuán jiégòu lái huàfēn
传统的酒店分类法是根据不同的市场定位和客源结构来划分
de, zhǔyào yǒu sì lèi: shāngwù jiǔdiàn, dùjià jiǔdiàn, gōngyù jiǔdiàn hé huìyì jiǔdiàn. Yòu
的，主要有四类：商务酒店、度假酒店、公寓酒店和会议酒店。又
gēnjù jiǔdiàn guīmó fēnwéi xiǎoxíng jiǔdiàn (kèfáng shùliàng zài 300 jiān yǐxià), zhōngxíng
根据酒店规模分为小型酒店（客房数量在300间以下）、中型
jiǔdiàn (kèfáng shùliàng zài 300~500 jiān) hé dàxíng jiǔdiàn (kèfáng shùliàng zài 500
酒店（客房数量在300～500间）和大型酒店（客房数量在500
jiān yǐshàng) děng.
间以上）等。

　　Hotels are traditionally classified into four major categories based on different market positioning and the structure of guest sources: business hotels, resort hotels, apartment hotels and conference hotels. According to the scale, hotels are divided into small hotels (with fewer than 300 guest rooms), medium-sized hotels (with 300-500 guest rooms) and large hotels (with more than 500 guest rooms).

第二部分　Part 2　汉字　Chinese Characters

一、汉字知识　Hànzì zhīshi　Knowledge about Chinese Characters

1. 汉字的笔画（1）　Strokes of Chinese characters (1)

笔画 Strokes	名称 Names	例字 Examples
一	横 héng	二
丨	竖 shù	十
丿	撇 piě	人
丶	捺 nà	八

2. 汉字的笔顺（1）　Stroke orders of Chinese characters (1)

规则 Rules	例字 Examples	笔顺 Stroke orders
先横后竖 Horizontal strokes before vertical strokes	十	一 十
先撇后捺 Left-falling strokes before right-falling strokes	人 八	丿 人 丿 八

二、汉字认读与书写　Hànzì rèndú yǔ shūxiě　The Recognition and Writing of Chinese Characters

认读下列词语，并试着读写构成词语的汉字。
Recognize the following words, and try to read and write the Chinese characters forming these words.

会议室　　洗衣房　　餐厅　　健身房

会			议			室			洗		
衣			房			餐			厅		
健			身			房					

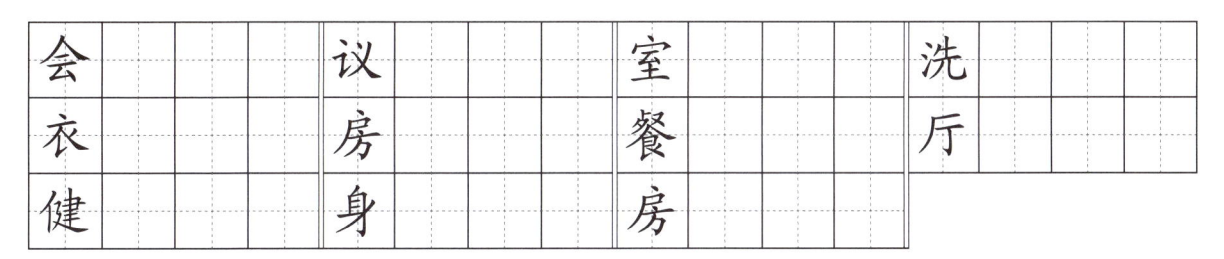

第三部分 Part 3 日常用语 Daily Expressions

1. 劳驾,帮我叫辆出租车。Láojià, bāng wǒ jiào liàng chūzūchē. Excuse me, please get me a taxi.
2. 明天见。Míngtiān jiàn. See you tomorrow.
3. 不见不散。Bújiàn-búsàn. Be there or be square.

第四部分 Part 4 单元实训 Unit Practical Training

模拟介绍酒店设施
Simulated Introduction to Hotel Facilities

实训目的 Training purpose

通过本次实训,了解并熟练掌握酒店基本设施的名称和功能。

Through the training, students will get to know and proficiently master the names and functions of basic hotel facilities.

实训组织 Training organization

每组2~4人

2-4 students in each group

实训内容 Training content

假设某公司要在酒店举行会议,需要预订会议室。在此之前,需要了解酒店是否有会议室、餐厅等,并了解各个设施的营业时间。

Suppose a company is going to book a conference room for a meeting. Prior to this, it's necessary to get to know whether the hotel has a conference room and a dining room, and the opening hours of each facility.

实训步骤 Training steps

1. 教师将实训教室分成若干个虚拟的酒店前台。

    The teacher divides the classroom into several mimetic hotel receptions.

2. 将参加实训的学员分成若干小组,每组2~4人。

    Divide the students into groups of 2-4.

3. 带领学员模拟客人询问酒店设施的情景,过程中给予学员适当帮助。

    Guide the students to make simulated conversations about hotel facilities and provide them with appropriate assistance during the process.

4. 小组成员轮流扮演客人和前台接待员,练习并表演对话。

    The group members take turns to play guests and receptionists, practicing and acting out the dialogs.

5. 教师总结评价,实训结束。

    The teacher makes a summary and evaluation, and ends the training.

第五部分　Part 5

单元小结　Unit Summary

词语 cíyǔ Vocabulary

普通词语　General Vocabulary

1.	喜欢	xǐhuan	v.	like
2.	尝	cháng	v.	try, taste
3.	食物	shíwù	n.	food
4.	楼	lóu	n.	floor
5.	午餐	wǔcān	n.	lunch
6.	晚餐	wǎncān	n.	supper
7.	游泳	yóuyǒng	v./n.	swim

专业词语　Specialized Vocabulary

1.	中餐厅	zhōngcāntīng	phr.	Chinese restaurant
2.	西餐厅	xīcāntīng	phr.	Western restaurant
3.	营业	yíngyè	v.	be open
4.	会议室	huìyìshì	n.	conference room
5.	游泳池	yóuyǒngchí	n.	swimming pool
6.	健身房	jiànshēnfáng	n.	gym

句子 jùzi Sentences

1. 我们有一个中餐厅和一个西餐厅。
2. 早餐从早上6点到10点，午餐从早上11点半到下午2点，晚餐从下午6点开始，9点半结束。
3. 祝您用餐愉快！
4. 洗衣房是免费使用的。
5. 会议室在三楼。
6. 您可以使用房间内提供的保险箱。

2

Tuánduì rùzhù dēngjì
团队入住登记
Group Check-in

tuánduì rùzhù dēngjì liúchéng
团队 入住登记流程
Group Check-in Process

jiēdàiyuán yào xúnwèn tuánduì de
接待员 要 询问 团队 的
míngchēng hé tuánhào
名称 和 团号
The receptionist asks the name and the number of the group

xiàng lǐngduì suǒyào kèrén míngdān
向 领队 索要客人名单
Asking for the name list of guests from the tour leader

bǎ páifángbiǎo gěi lǐngduì, ràng
把排房表 给领队,让
tā wèi kèrén fēnpèi fángjiān
他为客人分配房间
Giving the room allocation form to the tour leader and letting him allocate rooms for the guests

suǒyào tuánduì de hùzhào
索要 团队 的 护照
Asking for the passports of the group

bànlǐ dēngjì rùzhù
办理登记入住
Checking them in

13

题解　Introduction

1. 学习内容：酒店团队客人入住登记的流程和服务用语。
   Learning content: The process and service expressions for checking in a group of guests in a hotel.
2. 知识目标：掌握团队客人入住相关的核心词语，学习汉字的笔画"、""㇇""㇄""㇂"、笔顺"先上后下、先左后右"，学写本单元相关汉字。
   Knowledge objectives: To master the core vocabulary related to checking in a group of guests, learn the strokes "、", "㇇", "㇄", "㇂" and the stroke orders "upper strokes before lower strokes", "left-side strokes before right-side strokes" of Chinese characters, and write the characters related to this unit.
3. 技能目标：能正确处理团队客人入住时可能遇到的问题。
   Skill objective: To be able to properly handle problems that a group of guests may encounter when they check in.

第一部分　Part 1

课文 Texts

一、热身 rèshēn Warm-up

1. 给词语选择对应的图片。 Choose the corresponding pictures for the words.

A

B

C

D

　　lǚyóu qiānzhèng
❶ 旅游签证＿＿＿＿＿＿
　　tourist visa

　　lǚxíngtuán
❷ 旅行团＿＿＿＿＿＿
　　tour group

14

❸ tuánduì rùzhù zīliào dēngjìbiǎo
团队入住资料登记表_____
check-in form for a tour group

❹ bāshì
巴士_____
bus

2. 观看前台接待员办理团队客人入住登记的视频，对下列服务用语进行排序。
Watch the video about the receptionist checking in a group of guests. Arrange the following service expressions in order.

❶ Qǐng chūshì nín de hùzhào.
请 出示您的护照。
Your passport, please.

❷ Nín hǎo, yǒu shénme kěyǐ bāng nín?
您好，有什么可以帮您？
Hello, what can I do for you?

❸ Wǒ chádàole nǐmen de yùdìng jìlù, shí gè shuāngrénjiān, jīnwǎn rùzhù, duì ma?
我查到了你们的预订记录，十个 双人间，今晚入住，对吗？
I have got your booking record. Ten double rooms for tonight, right?

❹ Qǐng dēngjì yíxià tuánduì de zīliào.
请 登记一下 团队的资料。
Please register the information about your group.

❺ Zǎocān yíngyè shíjiān shì 6 diǎn, cāntīng zài sān lóu.
早餐 营业 时间 是6点，餐厅在三 楼。
Breakfast is served at 6:00 o'clock and the restaurant is on the third floor.

❻ Zhè shì nǐmen de fángkǎ hé zǎocānquàn.
这 是 你们的房卡和早餐券。
These are your room cards and breakfast vouchers.

二、课文 kèwén Texts

A 02-01

kèrén: 下午好，我想为我们团队办理入住。柬埔寨国际旅行社帮我们预订了八个房间。

qiántái jiēdàiyuán: 好的，先生。您能告诉我你们团队的名字吗？

kèrén: 中国旅行团。

qiántái jiēdàiyuán: 好的，您是领队吗？怎么称呼您？

kèrén: 是的，我叫李宁。

qiántái jiēdàiyuán: 李先生，我们已经查到你们团队的预订资料了。您的团队共有十位男士和六位女士，预订了八个双人间，其中有四对夫妇，对吗？团队成员现在都还在外面吗？

kèrén: 是的。他们还在巴士上。

团队入住登记
Group Check-in

前台 接待员: Nǐmen jiāng zài xīngqīwǔ tuì fáng, yǒu shénme biànhuà ma?
前台 接待员：你们 将 在星期五退房，有什么 变化 吗？

客人: Méiyǒu.
客人：没有。

前台 接待员: Hǎo de, Lǐ xiānsheng. Wǒ kěyǐ kànkan nǐmen de hùzhào ma?
前台 接待员：好的，李 先生。我可以 看看你们的护照 吗？

客人: Kěyǐ.
客人：可以。

前台 接待员: Qǐng tiánxiě tuánduì zīliào dēngjìbiǎo. Nǐmen de fángjiān zài dì 12 céng, zhè shì dài zǎocānquàn de fángkǎ.
前台 接待员：请 填写 团队资料登记表。你们的 房间 在第12层，这是带 早餐券 的房卡。

客人: Xièxie, nǐ néng wèi wǒmen ānpái zǎoshang 7 diǎn de jiàoxǐng diànhuà ma?
客人：谢谢，你能 为 我们安排 早上 7点的叫醒 电话 吗？

前台 接待员: Méi wèntí. Xíngliyuán huì bǎ xíngli sòngdào nǐmen de fángjiān, zhù nǐmen zhù de yúkuài!
前台 接待员：没问题。行李员会把行李 送到 你们的 房间，祝你们 住得愉快！

译文 yìwén Text in English

Guest: Good afternoon! I'd like to check in for our group. Cambodia International Travel Agency has booked eight rooms for us.
Receptionist: OK. Could you please tell me the name of your group?
Guest: China Travel Group.
Receptionist: All right. Are you the tour leader? May I have your name?
Guest: Yes, I am. My name is Li Ning.
Receptionist: Mr. Li, we've got the booking information of your group. Have you booked eight double rooms for ten men and six women, including four couples? Are all the group members still outside?
Guest: Yes. They are still on the bus.
Receptionist: You are going to check out on Friday. Will you change?
Guest: No, we won't.
Receptionist: Fine, Mr. Li. Can I see the passports of your group members?
Guest: Sure.
Receptionist: Please fill in the registration form for your group. Your rooms are on the 12th floor and these are the room cards with breakfast vouchers.
Guest: Thank you. Can you reserve a morning-call at 7 a.m. for us?
Receptionist: No problem. The porter will take the luggage to your rooms, and we wish you a pleasant stay!

普通词语 pǔtōng cíyǔ General Vocabulary 🎧 02-02

1.	团队	tuánduì	n.	team, group
2.	国际	guójì	n.	internationality
3.	名字	míngzi	n.	name
4.	称呼	chēnghu	v./n.	call; appellation
5.	资料	zīliào	n.	information, data
6.	共	gòng	adv.	altogether
7.	位	wèi	m.	a measure word used in deferential reference to people
8.	男士	nánshì	n.	man
9.	对	duì	m.	a measure word for people, animals, etc.
10.	夫妇	fūfù	n.	husband and wife, couple
11.	成员	chéngyuán	n.	member
12.	外面	wàimiàn	n.	outside
13.	巴士	bāshì	n.	bus
14.	上	shang	n.	used after a noun to indicate the surface of sth.
15.	将	jiāng	adv./prep.	used to indicate an imminent/a future occurrence; with, by
16.	星期五	xīngqīwǔ	n.	Friday
	星期	xīngqī	n.	week
17.	变化	biànhuà	v./n.	change
18.	填写	tiánxiě	v.	fill in
19.	第	dì	pref.	a prefix indicating ordinal numbers
20.	层	céng	m.	floor
21.	带	dài	v.	be with, have (sth.) attached

专业词语 zhuānyè cíyǔ Specialized Vocabulary 🎧 02-03

1.	柬埔寨	Jiǎnpǔzhài	pn.	Cambodia
2.	旅行社	lǚxíngshè	n.	travel agency
3.	中国	Zhōngguó	pn.	China
4.	旅行团	lǚxíngtuán	n.	travel group
5.	领队	lǐngduì	n.	(tour) leader
6.	登记表	dēngjìbiǎo	n.	registration form
7.	早餐券	zǎocānquàn	n.	breakfast voucher

团队入住登记
Group Check-in

B 🎧 02-04

客人：你好！我们团队在你们酒店预订了七间房，我是这个团队的领队王芳。

前台接待员：请稍等，我查一下我们的预订记录。你们团14个人，预订的是6月2日、3日两晚的七间海景房，是吗？

客人：是的，麻烦帮我办理入住。

前台接待员：当然可以，女士，我们已经准备好了登记表，麻烦出示一下你们团队14人的护照。

客人：好的，我们这边有统一的团队签证。

前台接待员：好的，我可以确认你们的离店时间吗？

客人：我们6月4日早上9点退房。

前台接待员：好的，请问你们要怎么付款呢？

客人：所有费用都由我们旅行社转账支付给你们酒店。

前台接待员：好的，你们的房间在同一层。这是你们的房卡和早餐券，请分给您的成员，请您在这里签上名字和电话号码，好吗？

客人：好的。

前台接待员：这是你们的证件，请收好。希望您在这里住得愉快！

19

kèrén: Hǎo de, xièxie.
客人：好的，谢谢。

译文 yìwén Text in English

Guest: Hello! Our group has booked seven rooms in your hotel. I am Wang Fang, the tour leader.
Receptionist: Just a moment, please. Let me check our booking record. Has your group booked seven sea view rooms for 14 people on June 2nd and 3rd?
Guest: Yes. Could you help me check in?
Receptionist: Certainly, madam. We have the registration form ready. Could you please show me the fourteen members' passports?
Guest: OK. We have a unified group visa here.
Receptionist: OK. May I confirm your check-out time?
Guest: We'll check out at 9:00 a.m. on June 4th.
Receptionist: All right. How will you make the payment?
Guest: All the fees will be transferred from our travel agency to your hotel.
Receptionist: OK. Your rooms are on the same floor. Here are your room cards and breakfast vouchers. Please distribute them to your members. Would you please sign your name and phone number here?
Guest: Sure.
Receptionist: Here are your credentials. Please keep them well. We wish you a pleasant stay!
Guest: OK, thank you.

普通词语 pǔtōng cíyǔ General Vocabulary 02-05

1.	麻烦	máfan	v./adj.	trouble; troublesome
2.	准备	zhǔnbèi	v.	prepare
3.	统一	tǒngyī	adj.	unified
4.	费用	fèiyong	n.	cost, fee
5.	由	yóu	prep.	by
6.	分给	fēn gěi	phr.	distribute
7.	签	qiān	v.	sign, write one's signature
8.	收好	shōuhǎo	phr.	keep well

专业词语 zhuānyè cíyǔ Specialized Vocabulary 02-06

1.	签证	qiānzhèng	n.	visa
2.	离店	lí diàn	phr.	check out
3.	付款	fùkuǎn	v.	pay a sum of money

| 4. | 转账 | zhuǎn//zhàng | v. | transfer accounts |
| 5. | 同一层 | tóng yì céng | phr. | the same floor |

三、视听说　shì-tīng-shuō　Viewing, Listening and Speaking

1. 观看前台接待员帮旅行团领队办理客人入住登记的视频，根据听到的内容选择正确选项，两人一组，模拟对话。

Watch the video about the receptionist helping a tour leader check in guests. Choose the right answers based on what you hear and simulate the conversation in pairs.

qiántái: Zǎoshang hǎo, qǐngwèn shéi shì lǐngduì?
前台：早上好，请问谁是领队？

lǐngduì: Wǒ.
领队：我。

qiántái: Nín hǎo, wǒ shì Lìli. Huānyíng rùzhù wǒmen jiǔdiàn, wǒ xiǎng quèrèn yíxià nín de rùzhù ānpái ①。
前台：您好，我是莉莉。欢迎入住我们酒店，我想确认一下您的入住安排 ①。

lǐngduì: Hǎo de.
领队：好的。

qiántái: Qǐngwèn rùzhù rénshù yǒu biànhuà ma? Xūyào rùzhù de ② yǒu biànhuà ma?
前台：请问入住人数有变化吗？需要入住的 ② 有变化吗？

lǐngduì: Méiyǒu.
领队：没有。

qiántái: Hǎo de, nín de tuì fáng shíjiān shì míngtiān shàngwǔ 9 diǎn, duì ma?
前台：好的，您的退房时间是明天上午9点，对吗？

lǐngduì: Wǒmen yào gǎi dào 9 diǎn 30 fēn.
领队：我们要改到9点30分。

qiántái: Nà yuánlái ānpái de zǎoshang 7 diǎn ③ xūyào gēnggǎi dào 7 diǎn 30 fēn ma?
前台：那原来安排的早上7点 ③ 需要更改到7点30分吗？

lǐngduì: Hǎo de.
领队：好的。

qiántái: Qǐngwèn nín néng ràng ④ zài míngtiān zǎoshang 9 diǎn qián jiāng xínglǐ fàngzài fángjiān ménkǒu ma?
前台：请问您能让 ④ 在明天早上9点前将行李放在房间门口吗？

Xínglǐyuán huì lái qǔ. Shìfǒu hái xūyào qítā fúwù ne?
行李员会来取。是否还需要其他服务呢？

lǐngduì: Méiyǒu le, jiù zhèxiē, xièxie.
领队：没有了，就这些，谢谢。

qiántái: Xièxiè, xīwàng nín zài zhèr guò de yúkuài!
前台：谢谢，希望您在这儿过得愉快！

jìhuàbiǎo A. 计划表 schedule	jiàozǎo fúwù B. 叫早服务 morning-call service	fángjiān lèixíng C. 房间类型 room type	tuánduì chéngyuán D. 团队成员 group member

2. 说一说 Let's talk.

练习说一说酒店前台接待人员办理团队客人入住时的工作流程。
Talk about a receptionist's workflow when he checks in a group of guests in a hotel.

四、学以致用 xuéyǐzhìyòng Practicing What You Have Learnt

观看前台接待员与旅行团领队确认团队入住信息的视频，根据团队入住登记表和房间类型及房号单，连线正确的团队入住信息。

Watch the video about the receptionist confirming the check-in information with the tour leader and match the right information according to the group check-in form, the room types, and the list of room numbers.

团体入住登记表 Group Check-in Form

团队编号：2021071700
Group No.:2021071700

tuántǐ míngchēng: Zhōngguó Lǚxíngtuán 团体名称：中国旅行团 Name of the group:	rénshù: 16 rén 人数：16人 Number of people:	fùkuǎn dānwèi: lǚxíngshè 付款单位：旅行社 Payer:
dàodá rìqī: 7 yuè 18 rì 到达日期：7月18日 Date of arrival:	líkāi rìqī: 7 yuè 19 rì 离开日期：7月19日 Date of departure:	shōu xíngli shíjiān: 7 yuè 19 rì 收行李时间：7月19日 zǎoshang 9 diǎn 早上9点 Luggage collection time:

团队入住登记 2
Group Check-in

（续表）

dìngjīn: 6000 yuán 订金：6000 元 Deposit:	fùkuǎn fāngshì: zhuǎnzhàng 付款方式：转账 Method of payment:	jiào xǐng shíjiān: zǎoshang 7 diǎn 30 fēn 叫醒时间：早上7点30分 Time for the morning call:
yòngcān yāoqiú: zǎocān 用餐要求：早餐 Meal requirements:		

房间类型及房号 Room Types and Room Numbers

fángjiān lèixíng 房间类型 Room types	fángjiān hàomǎ 房间号码 Room numbers	kèrén xìngmíng 客人姓名 Names of the guests	bèizhù 备注 Remarks
双人间	501		
双人间	502		
双人间	503		
双人间	504		
三人间	505		
行政套房	508		
单人间	506		
单人间	507		
zhìbiǎorén 制表人 Made by	Lǐ Huá 李华	péitóng qiānmíng 陪同签名 Guide's signature	Wáng Fāng 王芳
bèizhù 备注 Remarks		bèizhù 备注 Remarks	

信息确认 **Confirmation**

① dàodá rìqī
到达日期
Date of arrival

② líkāi rìqī
离开日期
Date of departure

A. zhuǎnzhàng
转账

B. zǎocān
早餐

23

③ 双人间 房间数
Number of double rooms

④ 付款方式
Method of payment

⑤ 用餐要求
Meal requirements

C. 7月18日

D. 四间

E. 7月19日

五、小知识 xiǎo zhīshi Tips

1. 前台接到团队入住通知单后，要根据接待单上的要求逐一核实房号、房间类型、付款方式、具体的抵离时间等；

2. 按照团队要求提前分配好房间；

3. 接待人员与领队确认房间数、人数及叫早时间、用餐要求；

4. 经确认后，请领队在团队接待单上签字，且前台接待人员也需在上面签字；

5. 手续办完后，前台接待人员将房号名单转交礼宾部，以便搬运行李；

6. 修正完所有更改事项后，及时将所有信息输入到电脑中。

    1. After receiving the check-in form of the group, the receptionist needs to check the room numbers, room types, method of payment, arrival and departure time and other information listed in the form;

    2. Allocate the rooms in advance as required by the group;

    3. The receptionist confirms the number of rooms, number of people, morning-call time and meal requirements with the tour leader;

    4. After confirmation, both the tour leader and the receptionist sign on the check-in form;

5. When finishing the formalities, the receptionist passes the list of room numbers on to the concierge department for luggage handling;

6. After modifying all the changes, input all the information into the computer in time.

第二部分　Part 2　汉字　Chinese Characters

一、汉字知识　Hànzì zhīshi　Knowledge about Chinese Characters

1. 汉字的笔画（2）Strokes of Chinese characters (2)

笔画 Strokes	名称 Names	例字 Examples
丶	点 diǎn	六
㇕	横折 héngzhé	口、日、五
㇄	竖折 shùzhé	山
㇜	撇折 piězhé	么

2. 汉字的笔顺（2）Stroke orders of Chinese characters (2)

规则 Rules	例字 Examples	笔顺 Stroke orders
先上后下 Upper strokes before lower strokes	三	一 二 三
先左后右 Left-side strokes before right-side strokes	人	丿 人

二、汉字认读与书写　Hànzì rèndú yǔ shūxiě　The Recognition and Writing of Chinese Characters

认读下列词语，并试着读写构成词语的汉字。
Recognize the following words, and try to read and write the Chinese characters forming these words.

旅行社　　转账支付　　团队签证

旅			行			社			转		
账			支			付			团		
队			签			证					

第三部分 Part 3 日常用语 Daily Expressions

① 最近怎么样？Zuìjìn zěnmeyàng? How are you doing these days?
② 认识您很高兴。Rènshi nín hěn gāoxìng. Nice to meet you.

第四部分 Part 4 单元实训 Unit Practical Training

模拟办理团体入住
Simulated Group Check-in

实训目的 Training purpose

通过本次实训，了解并熟练掌握前台接待旅行社领队，并办理团体入住登记的流程。

Through the training, students will get to know and proficiently master the process of receiving a tour leader and checking in a group.

实训组织 Training organization

每组 4 人

4 students in each group

实训内容 Training content

前台接待员为旅行社领队办理团队客人入住登记，确认入住时间、人数、行李情况、叫早服务、支付方式等。

The receptionist helps the tour leader check in a group of guests and confirms the check-in time, number of people, luggage, morning-call service, and method of payment, etc.

实训步骤 Training steps

① 教师将实训教室分成若干个虚拟的酒店前台。

The teacher divides the classroom into several mimetic hotel receptions.

② 将参加实训的学员分成若干小组，每组 4 人。

Divide the students into groups of four.

③ 带领学员模拟为旅行社领队办理团队客人入住登记的情景，确认入住时间、人数、行李情况、叫早服务、支付方式等，过程中给予学员适当帮助。

Guide the students to simulate the group check-in for the tour leader, confirming the check-in time, number of people, luggage, morning-call service, method of payment, etc. Provide them with appropriate assistance during the process.

④ 小组成员轮流扮演领队和前台接待员，练习并表演对话。

The group members take turns to play tour leaders and receptionists, practicing and acting out the dialogs.

❺ 教师总结评价，实训结束
The teacher makes a summary and evaluation, and ends the training.

第五部分　Part 5　单元小结　Unit Summary

cíyǔ
词语
Vocabulary

普通词语　General Vocabulary

1.	团队	tuánduì	n.	team, group
2.	国际	guójì	n.	internationality
3.	名字	míngzi	n.	name
4.	称呼	chēnghu	v./n.	call; appellation
5.	资料	zīliào	n.	information, data
6.	共	gòng	adv.	altogether
7.	位	wèi	m.	a measure word used in deferential reference to people
8.	男士	nánshì	n.	man
9.	对	duì	m.	a measure word for people, animals, etc.
10.	夫妇	fūfù	n.	husband and wife, couple
11.	成员	chéngyuán	n.	member
12.	外面	wàimiàn	n.	outside
13.	巴士	bāshì	n.	bus
14.	上	shang	n.	used after a noun to indicate the surface of sth.
15.	将	jiāng	adv./prep.	used to indicate an imminent/a future occurrence; with, by
16.	星期五	xīngqīwǔ	n.	Friday
	星期	xīngqī	n.	week
17.	变化	biànhuà	v./n.	change
18.	填写	tiánxiě	v.	fill in
19.	第	dì	pref.	a prefix indicating ordinal numbers
20.	层	céng	m.	floor
21.	带	dài	v.	be with, have (sth.) attached
22.	麻烦	máfan	v./adj.	trouble; troublesome
23.	准备	zhǔnbèi	v.	prepare
24.	统一	tǒngyī	adj.	unified

25.	费用	fèiyong	n.	cost, fee
26.	由	yóu	prep.	by
27.	分给	fēn gěi	phr.	distribute
28.	签	qiān	v.	sign, write one's signature
29.	收好	shōuhǎo	phr.	keep well

专业词语　Specialized Vocabulary

cíyǔ 词语 Vocabulary

1.	柬埔寨	Jiǎnpǔzhài	pn.	Cambodia
2.	旅行社	lǚxíngshè	n.	travel agency
3.	中国	Zhōngguó	pn.	China
4.	旅行团	lǚxíngtuán	n.	travel group
5.	领队	lǐngduì	n.	(tour) leader
6.	登记表	dēngjìbiǎo	n.	registration form
7.	早餐券	zǎocānquàn	n.	breakfast voucher
8.	签证	qiānzhèng	n.	visa
9.	离店	lí diàn	phr.	check out
10.	付款	fùkuǎn	v.	pay a sum of money
11.	转账	zhuǎn//zhàng	v.	transfer accounts
12.	同一层	tóng yì céng	phr.	the same floor

jùzi 句子 Sentences

1. 您能告诉我你们团队的名字吗？
2. 我查到了你们的预订记录，十个双人间，今晚入住。
3. 请登记一下团队的资料。
4. 这是你们的房卡和早餐券。
5. 我可以看看你们的护照吗？
6. 我可以确认你们的离店时间吗？
7. 请问你们要怎么付款呢？
8. 请您在这里签上名字和电话号码。
9. 这是你们的证件，请收好。
10. 请填写团队资料登记表。
11. 行李员会把行李送到你们的房间。

3

Diàohuàn fángjiān
调换房间
Changing into Another Room

diàohuàn fángjiān chǔlǐ liúchéng
调换 房间处理流程
Process of Changing into Another Room

liǎojiě huàn fáng yuányīn (zàoshēng, fángjiān shèshī
了解换房原因（噪声、房间设施
gùzhàng, fángjiān wèishēng zhuàngkuàng chà děng）
故障、房间卫生状况差等）
Getting to know the reasons for changing into another room (noise, malfunction of room facilities, poor sanitary conditions of the room, etc.)

rú yǒu héshì fángjiān, mǎnzú huàn fáng xūqiú
如有合适房间，满足换房需求
Changing into another room if there are suitable rooms available

xiūgǎi diànnǎo zhōng de zīliào
修改电脑中的资料
Modifying the information in the computer

biǎodá qiànyì
表达歉意
Making an apology

bànlǐ huàn fáng shǒuxù
办理换房手续
Going through the formalities

cúndàng
存档
Putting it on file

题解　Introduction

1. 学习内容：酒店调换房间的流程和服务用语。
   Learning content: The process and service expressions for changing into another hotel room.
2. 知识目标：掌握调换房间相关的核心词语，学习汉字的笔画"㇀""亅""丿""乚"、笔顺"先中间后两边、先外边后里边"，学写本单元相关汉字。
   Knowledge objectives: To master the core vocabulary related to changing into another room, learn the strokes " ㇀ ", " 亅 ", " 丿 ", " 乚 " and the stroke orders "strokes in the middle before those on both sides", "outside strokes before inside strokes" of Chinese characters, and write the characters related to this unit.
3. 技能目标：能正确处理客人调换房间的要求。
   Skill objective: To be able to properly handle a guest's request to change his/her room into another one.

第一部分　Part 1

课文　Texts

一、热身　rèshēn　Warm-up

1. 给词语选择对应的图片。 Choose the corresponding pictures for the words.

A

B

C

D

❶ zàoshēng
噪声_____
noise

❷ yàoshi
钥匙_____
key

❸ fángkǎ
房卡_____
room card

❹ xíngli
行李_____
luggage

30

调换房间 3
Changing into Another Room

2. 观看视频，根据视频内容对下列服务流程进行排序。
Watch the video and arrange the following service processes in order based on the video.

xúnwèn huàn fáng yuányīn
询问 换 房 原因
Inquiring about the Reason for Change a Room

qiántái xúnwèn yuányīn
A. 前台 询问 原因

The receptionist asks why.

tōngguò diànhuà cháxún, quèrèn yǒu kōngfáng kěyǐ diàohuàn
B. 通过 电话 查询，确认 有 空房 可以 调换

After making a phone inquiry, the receptionist finds that there are still vacant rooms available.

diàohuàn fángjiān chénggōng
C. 调换 房间 成功

The guest has successfully changed his room into another one.

kèrén yāoqiú diàohuàn fángjiān
D. 客人 要求 调换 房间

The guest wants to change his/her room into another one.

❶ _____ ❷ _____ ❸ _____ ❹ _____

二、课文 kèwén Texts

A 🎧 03-01

qiántái jiēdàiyuán: Nín hǎo, qǐngwèn yǒu shénme kěyǐ bāngdào nín?
前台 接待员： 您好，请问有什么可以帮到您？

kèrén: Nín hǎo, wǒ shì 303 fángjiān de kèrén, wǒ xiǎng diàohuàn yíxià fángjiān.
客人： 您好，我是303房间的客人，我想调换一下房间。

qiántái jiēdàiyuán: hǎo de 303 shì dàchuángfáng, qǐngwèn nín xiǎng huàn shénme fángjiān?
前台 接待员： 好的，303是大床房，请问您想换什么房间？

kèrén: Míngtiān yǒu kèhù lái fǎngwèn, wǒ xiǎng huàn yì jiān tàofáng.
客人： 明天有客户来访问，我想换一间套房。

qiántái jiēdàiyuán: Hǎo de, tàofáng zài liù lóu.
前台 接待员： 好的，套房在六楼。

kèrén: Qǐngwèn tàofáng yǒu huìkètīng ma?
客人： 请问套房有会客厅吗？

qiántái jiēdàiyuán: Shìde, tàofáng yǒu yì jiān huìkètīng.
前台 接待员： 是的，套房有一间会客厅。

kèrén: Hǎo de, qǐng bāng wǒ diàohuàn.
客人： 好的，请帮我调换。

qiántái jiēdàiyuán: Kèfáng de yuángōng huì lái bāng nín ná xíngli.
前台 接待员： 客房的员工会来帮您拿行李。

kèrén: Hǎo de, xièxie.
客人： 好的，谢谢。

qiántái jiēdàiyuán: Bú kèqi, qǐng nín zài fángjiān děnghòu.
前台 接待员： 不客气，请您在房间等候。

译文 yìwén Text in English

Receptionist: Hello, what can I do for you?

Guest: Hello, I'm the guest in Room 303. I'd like to change my room into another one.

Receptionist: OK, 303 is a queen room. What kind of room would you like to change into?

Guest: A client will visit me tomorrow, so I want to change into a suite.

Receptionist: OK, the suites are on the sixth floor.

Guest: Is there a living room in the suite?

Receptionist: Yes, there is.

Guest: OK. Please help me change to that one.

Receptionist: The guest room staff will help you with your luggage.

Guest: Thank you!

Receptionist: You're welcome. Please wait in your room.

调换房间 3
Changing into Another Room

普通词语 pǔtōng cíyǔ General Vocabulary 🎧 03-02

1.	客户	kèhù	n.	client
2.	访问	fǎngwèn	v.	visit
3.	员工	yuángōng	n.	staff
4.	等候	děnghòu	v.	wait

专业词语 zhuānyè cíyǔ Specialized Vocabulary 🎧 03-03

1.	调换	diàohuàn	v.	exchange, swap
2.	换	huàn	v.	exchange
3.	会客厅	huìkètīng	n.	living room
4.	客房	kèfáng	n.	guest room

B 🎧 03-04

客人 (kèrén): 你好，我想调换一下房间。
Nǐ hǎo, wǒ xiǎng diàohuàn yíxià fángjiān.

前台接待员 (qiántái jiēdàiyuán): 您好，请问是什么原因？
Nín hǎo, qǐngwèn shì shénme yuányīn?

客人 (kèrén): 我的房间对着马路，有点儿吵。
Wǒ de fángjiān duì zhe mǎlù, yǒudiǎnr chǎo.

前台接待员 (qiántái jiēdàiyuán): 好的，您预订的是城景房，我可以帮您换成园景房。
Hǎo de, nín yùdìng de shì chéngjǐngfáng, wǒ kěyǐ bāng nín huànchéng yuánjǐngfáng.

客人 (kèrén): 园景房在什么方向？
Yuánjǐngfáng zài shénme fāngxiàng?

前台接待员 (qiántái jiēdàiyuán): 园景房在城景房的反方向，面对酒店的花园。
Yuánjǐngfáng zài chéngjǐngfáng de fǎn fāngxiàng, miànduì jiǔdiàn de huāyuán.

客人 (kèrén): 好的，谢谢。
Hǎo de, xièxie.

前台接待员 (qiántái jiēdàiyuán): 不客气！
Bú kèqi!

译文 yìwén Text in English

Guest: Hello, I'd like to change my room into another one.
Receptionist: Hello, may I know the reason?

Guest: My room faces the road, so it's a bit noisy.

Receptionist: OK. You reserved a city view room. I can help you change into a garden view room.

Guest: In what direction is the garden view room?

Receptionist: It is opposite to the city view room, facing the garden of the hotel.

Guest: OK, thanks!

Receptionist: You're welcome!

普通词语 pǔtōng cíyǔ General Vocabulary 🎧 03-05

1.	原因	yuányīn	n.	reason
2.	对	duì	v.	towards
3.	马路	mǎlù	n.	road
4.	吵	chǎo	adj.	noisy
5.	方向	fāngxiàng	n.	direction
6.	反	fǎn	adj.	opposite
7.	面对	miànduì	v.	face
8.	花园	huāyuán	n.	garden

专业词语 zhuānyè cíyǔ Specialized Vocabulary 🎧 03-06

城景房	chéngjǐngfáng	n.	city view room

三、视听说 shì-tīng-shuō Viewing, Listening and Speaking

1. 观看前台接待员帮领队为团队客人调换房间的视频，根据听到的内容选择正确选项，两人一组，模拟对话。

Watch the video about the receptionist helping the tour leader change one of his guest's room into another one, choose the right answers based on what you hear, and simulate a conversation in pairs.

gènghuàn fángxíng
更换 房型
Chang Room Type

lǚxíngtuán lǐngduì: Nǐ hǎo! Wǒ shì Nánfāng Lǚxíngtuán de lǐngduì,
旅行团 领队　你好！我是 南方 旅行团的领队， ① 。

34

调换房间 3
Changing into Another Room

qiántái jiēdàiyuán: Qǐngwèn nín kèrén de míngzi shì?
前台 接待员：请问 您客人的名字 是？

lǚxíngtuán lǐngduì: Lǐ Lín.
旅行团 领队：李林。

qiántái jiēdàiyuán:
前台 接待员： ❷ 。

lǚxíngtuán lǐngduì: Fángjiānhào shì 303.
旅行团 领队：房间号 是 303。

qiántái jiēdàiyuán: Nín de kèrén yǐjīng yùdìngle yì jiān shuāngchuángfáng,
前台 接待员：您 的客人已经 预订了 一间 双床房， ❸ ?

lǚxíngtuán lǐngduì: Huànchéng dàchuángfáng.
旅行团 领队：换成 大床房。

qiántái jiēdàiyuán: Hǎo de, wǒ bāng nín diàohuàn,
前台 接待员：好的，我 帮 您 调换， ❹ 。

lǚxíngtuán lǐngduì: Xièxie!
旅行团 领队：谢谢！

zhè shì nín de xīn fángkǎ
A. 这是您的新房卡
This is your new room card.

wǒ xiǎng bāng wǒ de kèrén diàohuàn yíxià fángjiān
B. 我 想 帮 我的客人 调换 一下 房间
I'd like to change the room into another one for my guest.

qǐngwèn nín kèrén de fángjiānhào
C. 请问 您客人的房间号
May I have your guest's room number?

qǐngwèn yào huànchéng shénme fángxíng
D. 请问 要 换成 什么 房型
What kind of room would you like to change into?

2. 说一说　Let's talk.

练习说一说调换房间的步骤。　Talk about the steps of changing rooms.

四、学以致用　xuéyǐzhìyòng　Practicing What You Have Learnt

diàohuàn fángjiān
调换 房间
Changing Rooms

Wǒmen xuéxíle jiǔdiàn gèzhǒng fángjiān lèixíng, xiànzài jiǎshè nǐ shì Guāngmíng Lǚxíngtuán de lǐngduì,
我们 学习了酒店 各种 房间 类型，现在 假设你是 光明 旅行团的领队，

35

酒店前台将一号家庭（一对夫妻）分在了B房间，二号家庭（三口之家）分在了C房间，三号家庭（四口之家）分在了A房间。你发现这样不合适，请为他们调换房间。

We've learnt about various hotel room types. Now suppose you are the tour leader of Guangming Tour Group. The hotel receptionist assigns Room B to Family No. __1__, Room C to Family No. __2__, and Room A to Family No. __3__. You realize it's not appropriate. Please swap rooms for your guests.

A　　　　　　　　　　B　　　　　　　　　　C

❶ _____　　　　❷ _____　　　　❸ _____

五、小知识　xiǎo zhīshi　Tips

如何应对客人调换房间的要求

前台在入住登记时应询问清楚客人的特殊要求，有针对性地给客人安排房间。当客人要求换房时，前台需询问换房原因。如果是因为设备故障，且短时间内可以修复，就尽量不换，争取得到客人谅解。办理换房手续时要更换相应房卡或房间钥匙；填写相应的"房间/房价变更通知单"，客人签字确认后，酒店前台和客人各自保留一份通知单。

How to Respond to a Guest's Request to Change His/Her Room into Another One

When the guest checks in, the receptionist should inquire about his/her special requirements about the room and arranges a room based on his/her needs. When a guest asks for changing his/her room into

调换房间 3
Changing into Another Room

another one, the receptionist needs to inquire about the reason for the change. If it is due to equipment malfunction and can be fixed in a short time, try not to change the room into another one and to get the guest's understanding. When handling the procedures, receptionist should change the corresponding room card or room key and fill out the "Room/Room Rate Change Notice". After the guest signs and confirms, both the hotel receptionist and the guest keep a copy of the notice.

第二部分　Part 2　　汉字　Chinese Characters

一、汉字知识　Hànzì zhīshi　Knowledge about Chinese Characters

1. 汉字的笔画（3）　Strokes of Chinese characters (3)

笔画 Strokes	名称 Names	例字 Examples
⏋	横钩 hénggōu	买
亅	竖钩 shùgōu	小
㇁	弯钩 wāngōu	子
㇄	竖弯钩 shùwāngōu	七

2. 汉字的笔顺（3）　Stroke orders of Chinese characters (3)

规则 Rules	例字 Examples	笔顺 Stroke orders
先中间后两边 Strokes in the middle before those on both sides	小	亅 小 小
先外边后里边 Outside strokes before inside strokes	问	` 冂 门 闩 问 问

二、汉字认读与书写　Hànzì rèndú yǔ shūxiě　The Recognition and Writing of Chinese Characters

认读下列词语，并试着读写构成词语的汉字。
Recognize the following words, and try to read and write the Chinese characters forming these words.

调换　　会客厅　　行李　　城景房

调				换				会				客			
厅				行				李				城			
景				房											

37

第三部分 Part 3　日常用语 Daily Expressions

❶ 我来介绍一下，这位是李伟先生。Wǒ lái jièshào yíxià, zhè wèi shì Lǐ Wěi xiānsheng. Let me make an introduction. This is Mr. Li Wei.

❷ 请问，南京饭店在哪儿？ Qǐngwèn, Nánjīng Fàndiàn zài nǎr? Excuse me, where's Nanjing Hotel?

第四部分 Part 4　单元实训 Unit Practical Training

模拟调换房间
Simulated Changing into Another Room

实训目的 Training purpose
通过本次实训，了解并熟练掌握酒店调换房间的步骤流程和服务用语。
Through the training, students will get to know and proficiently master the steps of changing a guest's room into another one in a hotel and the service expressions used during the process.

实训组织 Training organization
每组 2～3 人
2-3 students in each group

实训内容 Training content
某酒店客人因噪声困扰需要调换房间，前台经过核实后，成功帮该客人调换房间。
A guest in a hotel needs to change his/her room into another one due to the noise. After verification, the receptionist helps the guest make it.

实训步骤 Training steps
❶ 教师将实训教室分成若干个虚拟的酒店前台。
   The teacher divides the classroom into several mimetic hotel receptions.
❷ 将参加实训的学员分成若干小组，每组 2～3 人。
   Divide the students into groups of 2-3.
❸ 带领学员模拟调换房间的步骤流程，过程中给予学员适当帮助。
   Guide the students to simulate the process of changing into another room, and provide them with appropriate assistance during the process.
❹ 小组成员轮流扮演客人和前台接待员，练习并表演对话。
   The group members take turns to play guests and receptionists, practicing and acting out the dialogs.
❺ 教师总结评价，实训结束。
   The teacher makes a summary and evaluation, and ends the training.

第五部分　Part 5

单元小结　Unit Summary

词语 Vocabulary

普通词语　General Vocabulary

1.	客户	kèhù	n.	client
2.	访问	fǎngwèn	v.	visit
3.	员工	yuángōng	n.	staff
4.	等候	děnghòu	v.	wait
5.	原因	yuányīn	n.	reason
6.	对	duì	v.	towards
7.	马路	mǎlù	n.	road
8.	吵	chǎo	adj.	noisy
9.	方向	fāngxiàng	n.	direction
10.	反	fǎn	adj.	opposite
11.	面对	miànduì	v.	face
12.	花园	huāyuán	n.	garden

专业词语　Specialized Vocabulary

1.	调换	diàohuàn	v.	exchange, swap
2.	换	huàn	v.	exchange
3.	会客厅	huìkètīng	n.	living room
4.	客房	kèfáng	n.	guest room
5.	城景房	chéngjǐngfáng	n.	city view room

句子 Sentences

1. 请问您想换什么房间？
2. 请问是什么原因？
3. 客房的员工会来帮您拿行李。
4. 请您在房间等候。
5. 我可以帮您换成园景房。
6. 园景房在城景房的反方向，面对酒店的花园。

4

Xù zhù fúwù
续住服务
Extended-Stay Service

xù zhù fúwù liúchéng
续住服务流程
Extended-Stay Service Process

quèrèn fángtài
确认 房态
Confirming the status of the room

héshí xù zhù xìnxī
核实续住信息
Checking the extended-stay information with the guest

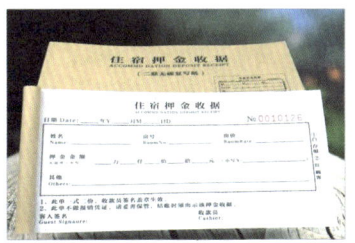

chákàn kèrén yājīn zhuàngtài
查看客人押金状态
Checking the status of the deposit from the guest

bànlǐ xù zhù shǒuxù
办理续住手续
Going through the extended-stay procedures

gēngxīn fángkǎ
更新 房卡
Updating the room card

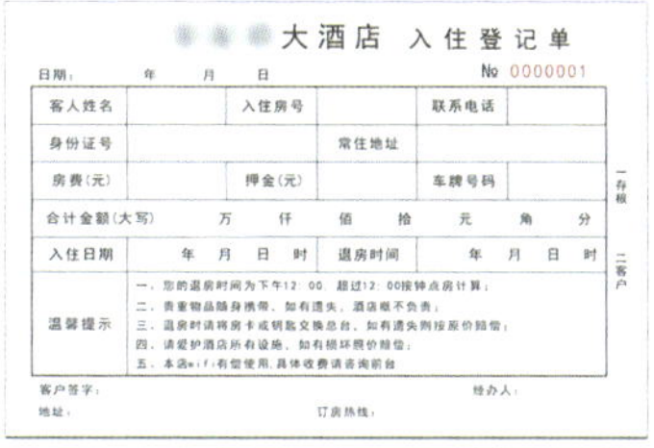

gēnggǎi rùzhù dēngjìdān
更改 入住登记单
Changing the check-in form

41

题解　Introduction

1. 学习内容：酒店续住服务的流程和服务用语。
   Learning content: The process and service expressions for extended-stay service in a hotel.
2. 知识目标：掌握续住服务相关的核心词语，学习汉字的笔画 "㇀" "㇂" "㇉" "㇁"、笔顺 "先外后里再封口"，学写本单元相关汉字。
   Knowledge objectives: To master the core vocabulary related to extended-stay service, learn the strokes "㇀", "㇂", "㇉", "㇁" and the stroke order "Outside strokes before inside strokes, and then sealing strokes" of Chinese characters, and write the characters related to this unit.
3. 技能目标：能正确处理客人的续住要求，并为客人办理续住。
   Skill objective: To be able to handle a guest's extended-stay request and go through the formalities for him/her.

第一部分　Part 1

课文　Texts

一、热身　rèshēn　Warm-up

1. 给词语选择对应的图片。 Choose the corresponding pictures for the words.

A

B

C

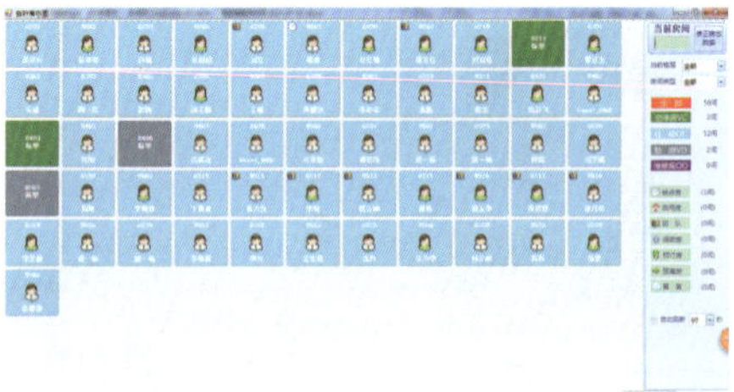

D

　　yājīndān
❶ 押金单＿＿＿＿＿＿＿＿
deposit receipt

　　fángtài qíngkuàng
❷ 房态　情况＿＿＿＿＿＿＿＿
status of the rooms

　　zhìzuò fángkǎ
❸ 制作 房卡＿＿＿＿＿＿＿＿
making the room card

　　kèmǎn
❹ 客满＿＿＿＿＿＿＿＿
fully booked

续住服务 4
Extended-Stay Service

2. 观看视频，根据视频内容对下列服务流程进行排序。
Watch the video and arrange the following service process in order based on the video.

办理 续住
bànlǐ xù zhù
Stay Extension

jiǔdiàn yǒu kōngfáng kěyǐ xù zhù, kèrén xūyào zàicì yùfù yājīn
A. 酒店有空房可以续住，客人需要再次预付押金
The hotel has vacant rooms available for extended stay, and the guest needs to prepay a deposit again.

qiántái jiāng chóngxīn zhìzuò fángkǎ
B. 前台将重新制作房卡
The receptionist will make a new room card.

qiántái jiēdàiyuán quèrèn fángtài qíngkuàng
C. 前台接待员确认房态情况
The receptionist confirms the room status.

kèrén xiǎng yào bànlǐ xù zhù
D. 客人想要办理续住
The guest wants to extend his stay.

chénggōng bànlǐ xù zhù
E. 成功办理续住
The guest has successfully extended his stay.

① _____ ② _____ ③ _____ ④ _____ ⑤ _____

二、课文　kèwén　Texts

A 🎧 04-01

kèrén: 客人:	Nǐ hǎo, wǒ xiǎng bànlǐ xù zhù. 你好，我想办理续住。	
qiántái jiēdàiyuán: 前台 接待员:	Hǎo de, qǐngwèn nín de xìngmíng hé fánghào? 好的，请问您的姓名和房号？	
kèrén: 客人:	Wáng Yí, fánghào shì 1305. 王仪，房号是1305。	

qiántái jiēdàiyuán héshí kèrén xìnxī, cháxún yú'é.
（前台 接待员 核实 客人 信息、查询 余额。）

qiántái jiēdàiyuán: 前台 接待员:	Qǐngwèn nín hái yào xù zhù jǐ tiān? 请问您还要续住几天？	
kèrén: 客人:	Liǎng tiān. 两天。	
qiántái jiēdàiyuán: 前台 接待员:	Qǐngwèn nín shì fù xiànjīn háishi shuā xìnyòngkǎ? 请问您是付现金还是刷信用卡？	
kèrén: 客人:	Xiànjīn. 现金。	
qiántái jiēdàiyuán: 前台 接待员:	Qǐng nín yùfù 500 yuán, xièxie. Zhè shì nín de fángkǎ hé yājīn shōujù, 请您预付500元，谢谢。这是您的房卡和押金收据，	
	qǐng shōuhǎo. Gǎnxiè nín de xù zhù, zhù nín yúkuài! 请收好。感谢您的续住，祝您愉快！	
kèrén: 客人:	Xièxie! 谢谢！	

译文 yìwén Text in English

Guest: Hello! I'd like to extend my stay.

Receptionist: OK! May I have your name and room number?

Guest: Wang Yi, and my room number is 1305.

(The receptionist is verifying the information about the guest and checking the account balance.)

Receptionist: How many more days would you like to stay?

Guest: Two days.

Receptionist: Would you like to pay in cash or by credit card?

Guest: Cash.

Receptionist: Please prepay 500 *yuan*, thanks. There are your room card and deposit receipt. Please keep them well. Thanks for the extension of your stay. Have a nice day!

Guest: Thank you!

4 Extended-Stay Service

续住服务

普通词语 pǔtōng cíyǔ General Vocabulary 🎧 04-02

1.	核实	héshí	v.	verify
2.	余额	yú'é	n.	balance, remaining sum
3.	付	fù	v.	pay
4.	现金	xiànjīn	n.	cash
5.	元	yuán	m.	*yuan* (the basic unit of money in China)

专业词语 zhuānyè cíyǔ Specialized Vocabulary 🎧 04-03

1.	续住	xù zhù	phr.	extended stay
2.	预付	yùfù	v.	prepay
3.	押金	yājīn	n.	deposit
4.	收据	shōujù	n.	receipt

B 🎧 04-04

kèrén:
客人: Nǐ hǎo, wǒ xiǎng yào bànlǐ xù zhù.
你好，我想要办理续住。

qiántái jiēdàiyuán:
前台 接待员: Qǐngwèn nín de fángjiānhào shì duōshao?
请问您的房间号是多少？

kèrén:
客人: 601. Wǒ běnlái dǎsuàn jīntiān tuì fáng de, dàn xiànzài wǒ xiǎng duō zhù yì tiān.
601。我本来打算今天退房的，但现在我想多住一天。

qiántái jiēdàiyuán:
前台 接待员: Qǐng shāo děng.
请稍等。

kèrén:
客人: Hǎo de.
好的。

qiántái jiēdàiyuán:
前台 接待员: Bù hǎoyìsi, xiānsheng. Nín de fángjiān míngtiān yǐjīng bèi yùdìng le.
不好意思，先生。您的房间明天已经被预订了。
Nín jièyì huàn yí gè fángjiān ma?
您介意换一个房间吗？

kèrén:
客人: Kěyǐ.
可以。

qiántái jiēdàiyuán:
前台 接待员: Gǎnxiè nín de lǐjiě. Máfan nín yíhuìr dào qiántái lái bànlǐ xù zhù shēnqǐng, bìng lǐngqǔ nín de xīn fángkǎ.
感谢您的理解。麻烦您一会儿到前台来办理续住申请，并领取您的新房卡。

45

译文 yìwén Text in English

Guest: Hello, I'd like to extend my stay.
Receptionist: May I know your room number, please?
Guest: 601, and I was supposed to check out today. But now I'd like to stay one more day.
Receptionist: Please wait a moment.
Guest: OK.
Receptionist: Sorry, sir. Your room has been booked for tomorrow. Would you mind changing into another room?
Guest: No.
Receptionist: Thanks for your understanding. Please apply for an extended stay at the information counter later and get your new room card.

普通词语 pǔtōng cíyǔ General Vocabulary 🎧 04-05

1.	本来	běnlái	adj./adv.	original; originally
2.	打算	dǎsuàn	v.	plan, intend
3.	不好意思	bù hǎoyìsi	phr.	sorry
4.	介意	jiè//yì	v.	mind
5.	感谢	gǎnxiè	v.	thank
6.	理解	lǐjiě	v.	understand
7.	领取	lǐngqǔ	v.	collect, pick up

专业词语 zhuānyè cíyǔ Specialized Vocabulary 🎧 04-06

申请	shēnqǐng	v.	apply

三、视听说 shì-tīng-shuō Viewing, Listening and Speaking

1. 观看前台接待员为客人办理续住的视频，根据听到的内容选择正确选项，两人一组，模拟对话。
Watch the video about the receptionist handling the guest's request for extended stay. Choose the right answers based on what you hear and simulate the conversation in pairs.

xù zhù xiétiáo
续住 协调
Extended stay coordination

续住服务 4
Extended-Stay Service

客人：你好，我想办理续住。

前台接待员：先生，请问您的姓名和房号？

客人：李明，1505房间。

前台接待员： ① 。

客人：我想再住两天。

前台接待员：请稍等， ② 。

客人：好的，谢谢。

前台接待员：先生， ③ ，我们明天将有两个旅行团到达，他们预订了15层的所有房间。

客人：那怎么办呢？

前台接待员： ④ ，我们可以为您安排。

客人：那太好了，谢谢你。

A. 我查一下后两天的客房住宿情况

Let me check the room status for the next two days.

B. 让您久等了

Sorry for keeping you waiting for such a long time.

C. 请问您想再住多久

How long would you like to extend your stay?

D. 如果您愿意搬到其他楼层的房间

If you don't mind moving into a room on another floor.

47

2. 说一说　Let's talk.

练习说一说为客人办理续住的流程。　Talk about the procedure of extending the stay for a guest.

四、学以致用　xuéyǐzhìyòng　Practicing What You Have Learnt

将下列服务用语进行排序。　Arrange the following service expressions in order.

填写行李牌
Fill in the Luggage Tag

① Xūyào wǒ wèi nín liánxì biéde jiǔdiàn ma?
需要 我 为 您 联系 别的 酒店 吗？
Shall I contact another hotel for you?

② Nǐ hǎo, wǒ shì 1508 de kèrén, xiǎng bànlǐ xù zhù.
你好，我是1508的客人，想 办理续住。
Hello! I'm the guest in Room 1508 and I'd like to extend my stay.

③ Yì zhōu.
一周。
One week.

④ Qǐngwèn nín xiǎng xù zhù jǐ tiān ne?
请问 您 想 续住几天 呢？
How many more days would you like to stay?

⑤ Tài yíhàn le!
太遗憾了！
What a pity!

⑥ Qǐng shāo děng, wǒ lái cháxún yíxià kèfáng zhùsù qíngkuàng. Ràng nín jiǔděng le, yīnwèi xiànzài shì lǚyóu wàngjì, jiǔdiàn méiyǒu kòngyú fángjiān, hěn bàoqiàn!
请 稍 等，我来查询一下客房住宿 情况。让 您久等了，因为现在是旅游旺季，酒店没有 空余 房间，很抱歉！
Please wait a moment. Let me check the room status. Sorry for having kept you waiting for such a long time. There are no vacancies in our hotel since it's the peak tourist season now.

续住服务
Extended-Stay Service 4

❼ Búyòng le, xièxie!
不用 了，谢谢！
No, thank you!

□ ➡ □ ➡ □ ➡ □ ➡ □ ➡ □

五、小知识　xiǎo zhīshi　Tips

Jiǔdiàn xù zhù
酒店续住

Zài yǒu fángjiān de qíngkuàng xià, jiǔdiàn huì bāngzhù kèrén xù fáng. Tōngcháng kèrén hái
在 有 房间的 情况 下，酒店会 帮助 客人续房。通常 客人还

huì zhù dāngqián de fángjiān, yīnwèi huànfáng chéngběn jiào gāo, ér xù zhù chéngběn jiào dī.
会住 当前 的 房间，因为 换 房 成本 较 高，而续住 成本 较低。

Lìngwài, jiǔdiàn yìbān huì jǐnliàng mǎnzú kèrén xù zhù xūqiú, yīnwèi xù zhù néng bǎozhèng
另外，酒店 一般 会 尽量 满足 客人续住需求，因为续住能 保证

dìngfángliàng, ér yùdìng zǒng yǒu yídìng qǔxiāo bǐlì. Tōngchánglái shuō, xù zhù dōu huì chénggōng.
订房量，而预订总 有一定 取消比例。通常 来说，续住都会 成功。

Extended-Stay in a Hotel

If there is a room available, the hotel will help the guest extend his/her stay. The guest will usually stay in the current room since the cost of changing his/her room into another one is higher than continuing to stay in the same room. In addition, the hotel will try not to let an extended-stay guest check out, since extended-stay can guarantee the booking volume, and there are always a certain proportion of cancellations for bookings. Extended-stay is usually approved.

第二部分　Part 2
汉字　Chinese Characters

一、汉字知识　Hànzì zhīshi　Knowledge about Chinese Characters

1. 汉字的笔画（4）　Strokes of Chinese characters (4)

笔画 Strokes	名称 Names	例字 Examples
㇀	提 tí	习
㇙	竖提 shùtí	衣
㇆	横折提 héngzhétí	语
㇇	撇点 piědiǎn	女

49

2. 汉字的笔顺（4） Stroke orders of Chinese characters (4)

规则 Rule	例字 Examples	笔顺 Stroke orders
先外后里再封口 Outside strokes before inside strokes, and then sealing strokes	国 日	丨 冂 冂 冂 冃 囯 国 国 丨 冂 冃 日

二、汉字认读与书写　Hànzì rèndú yǔ shūxiě　The Recognition and Writing of Chinese Characters

认读下列词语，并试着读写构成词语的汉字。
Recognize the following words, and try to read and write the Chinese characters forming these words.

续住　　现金　　申请　　账户

| 续 | | | 住 | | | 现 | | | 金 | | |
| 申 | | | 请 | | | 账 | | | 户 | | |

第三部分　Part 3
日常用语　Daily Expressions

❶ 我们机场见。Wǒmen jīchǎng jiàn. See you at the airport.
❷ 我们电话（邮件）联系。Wǒmen diànhuà (yóujiàn) liánxì. Keep in touch by phone (e-mail).
❸ 下星期一到北京的航班还有票吗？Xià xīngqīyī dào Běijīng de hángbān hái yǒu piào ma?
Are there any tickets available for next Monday's flight to Beijing?

第四部分　Part 4
单元实训　Unit Practical Training

模拟续住服务
Simulated Extended-Stay Service

实训目的 Training purpose

通过本次实训，了解并熟练掌握酒店续住服务的步骤流程和服务用语。
Through the training, students will get to know and proficiently master the steps of handling the extended-stay in a hotel and the service expressions used during the process.

实训组织 Training organization

每组 2～3 人

2-3 students in each group

实训内容 Training content

某酒店客人想要办理续住，前台查看房表后，成功帮该客人办理续住。

A guest in a hotel wants to extend his stay. After checking the room status, the receptionist helps him/her make it.

实训步骤 Training steps

❶ 教师将实训教室分成若干个虚拟的酒店前台。

The teacher divides the classroom into several mimetic hotel receptions.

❷ 将参加实训的学员分成若干小组，每组 2～3 人。

Divide the students into groups of 2-3.

❸ 带领学员模拟续住办理的情景，过程中给予学员适当帮助。

Guide the students to simulate extended-stay service, and provide them with appropriate help during the process.

❹ 小组成员轮流扮演客人和前台接待员，练习并表演对话。

The group members take turns to play guests and receptionists, practicing and acting out the dialogs.

❺ 教师总结评价，实训结束。

The teacher makes a summary and evaluation, and ends the training.

第五部分　Part 5　单元小结 Unit Summary

cíyǔ 词语 Vocabulary

普通词语　General Vocabulary

1.	核实	héshí	v.	verify
2.	余额	yú'é	n.	balance, remaining sum
3.	付	fù	v.	pay
4.	现金	xiànjīn	n.	cash
5.	元	yuán	m.	*yuan* (the basic unit of money in China)
6.	本来	běnlái	adj./adv.	original; originally
7.	打算	dǎsuàn	v.	plan, intend
8.	不好意思	bù hǎoyìsi	phr.	sorry
9.	介意	jiè//yì	v.	mind
10.	感谢	gǎnxiè	v.	thank

	11.	理解	lǐjiě	v.	understand
	12.	领取	lǐngqǔ	v.	collect, pick up

**cíyǔ
词语
Vocabulary**

专业词语　Specialized Vocabulary

1.	续住	xù zhù	phr.	extended stay
2.	预付	yùfù	v.	prepay
3.	押金	yājīn	n.	deposit
4.	收据	shōujù	n.	receipt
5.	申请	shēnqǐng	v.	apply

**jùzi
句子
Sentences**

1. 请问您还要续住几天？
2. 请问您是付现金还是刷信用卡？
3. 请您预付500元。
4. 这是您的房卡和押金收据，请收好。
5. 感谢您的续住，祝您愉快！
6. 抱歉，您的房间明天已经被预订了。
7. 您介意换一个房间吗？
8. 麻烦您一会儿到前台来办理续住申请。
9. 请领取您的新房卡。

5

Xíngli fúwù
行李服务
Luggage Service

xíngli jìcún liúchéng
行李寄存流程
Luggage Deposit Process

quèrèn shēnfèn
确认 身份
Confirming the guest's identity

jiǎnchá xíngli
检查 行李
Checking the luggage

xíngli lǐngqǔ
行李 领取
Claiming the luggage

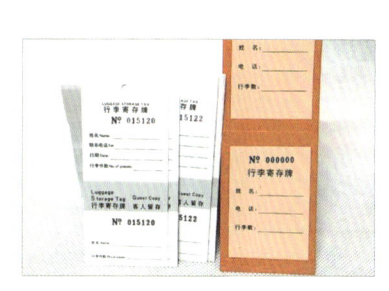

qǐng kèrén tiánxiě "jìcúnkǎ" bìng qiānmíng
请 客人 填写 "寄存卡" 并 签名
Asking the guest to fill in the "claim tag" and sign on it

yǒuxù bǎifàng xíngli
有序摆放行李
Putting the luggage in order

53

题解 Introduction

1. 学习内容：酒店行李服务的流程和服务用语。
   Learning content: The process and service expressions for luggage service in a hotel.
2. 知识目标：掌握行李服务相关的核心词语，学习汉字的笔画"㇏""㇋""亅""乚"和独体结构，学写本单元相关汉字。
   Knowledge objectives: To master the core vocabulary related to luggage service, learn the strokes "㇏", "㇋", "亅", "乚" and independent structure of Chinese characters, and write the characters related to this unit.
3. 技能目标：能为客人提供行李服务。
   Skill objectives: To be able to provide luggage service for a guest.

第一部分 Part 1

课文 Texts

一、热身 rèshēn Warm-up

1. 给词语选择对应的图片。 Choose the corresponding pictures for the words.

A

B

C

D

xíngliyuán
❶ 行李员＿＿＿＿＿＿＿
porter

xínglifáng
❷ 行李房＿＿＿＿＿＿＿
luggage room

sòng xíngli
❸ 送行李＿＿＿＿＿＿＿
luggage delivery

xínglijià
❹ 行李架＿＿＿＿＿＿＿
luggage rack

行李服务
Luggage Service

2. 观看视频，根据视频内容选择正确选项。
Watch the video and choose the right answers based on the video.

① xúnwèn qiántái xínglǐ fúwù
询问 前台 行李服务＿＿＿＿＿
ask the receptionist about luggage service

② kèrén bànlǐ rùzhù
客人办理入住＿＿＿＿＿
check in the guest

③ tiánxiě xínglipái
填写行李牌＿＿＿＿＿
fill in the luggage tag

④ jiāofù xínglǐ
交付行李＿＿＿＿＿
deliver the luggage

A. B. C. D.

二、课文　kèwén　Texts

A 🎧 05-01

kèrén: Nǐ hǎo, kěyǐ jiāng wǒ de xínglǐ sòngdào wǒ de fángjiān ma?
客人：你好，可以将 我的行李 送到 我的房间 吗？

55

lǐbīnyuán: 礼宾员：	Hǎo de, shì xiànzài sòng háishi qítā shíjiān ne? 好的，是现在送还是其他时间呢？	
kèrén: 客人：	Guò bàn gè xiǎoshí hòu. 过半个小时后。	
lǐbīnyuán: 礼宾员：	Hǎo de, máfan nín tiánxiě xínglipái. 好的，麻烦您填写行李牌。	
kèrén: 客人：	Hǎo de. 好的。	
lǐbīnyuán: 礼宾员：	Suíhòu wǒmen huì ānpái xínglìyuán jiāng nín de xíngli sòngdào nín de fángjiān. 随后我们会安排行李员将您的行李送到您的房间。	
kèrén: 客人：	Xièxie. 谢谢。	

译文 yìwén Text in English

Guest: Hello! Can you deliver my luggage to my room?
Concierge: OK, now or at some other time?
Guest: In half an hour.
Concierge: All right, please fill in the luggage tag.
Guest: All right.
Concierge: Then we will arrange a porter to deliver your luggage to your room.
Guest: Thanks.

普通词语 pǔtōng cíyǔ General Vocabulary 🎧 05-02

1.	其他	qítā	pron.	other
2.	过	guò	v.	spend (time), pass (time)
3.	随后	suíhòu	adv.	then

专业词语 zhuānyè cíyǔ Specialized Vocabulary 🎧 05-03

| 行李员 | xínglìyuán | n. | porter |

B 🎧 05-04

kèrén: 客人：	Nǐ hǎo, wǒ xiǎng jìcún xíngli. 你好，我想寄存行李。	
qiántái jiēdàiyuán: 前台接待员：	Qǐngwèn nín yào jìcún jǐ jiàn xíngli? 请问您要寄存几件行李？	

56

kèrén: 客人：	Liǎng gè xínglixiāng. 两 个 行李箱。	
qiántái jiēdàiyuán: 前台 接待员：	Qǐngwèn nín de xínglixiāng zhōng yǒu guìzhòng wùpǐn ma? 请问 您的行李箱 中 有 贵重 物品吗？	
kèrén: 客人：	Méiyǒu. 没有。	
qiántái jiēdàiyuán: 前台 接待员：	Qǐngwèn nín de xìngmíng hé fángjiānhào? 请问 您的 姓名 和房间号？	
kèrén: 客人：	Wáng Yí, 1606. 王 仪，1606。	
qiántái jiēdàiyuán: 前台 接待员：	Qǐngwèn nín shénme shíhou lái qǔ? 请问 您 什么 时候 来取？	
kèrén: 客人：	Jīntiān xiàwǔ 5 diǎn zuǒyòu. 今天 下午 5 点 左右。	
qiántái jiēdàiyuán: 前台 接待员：	1606 hào fángjiān Wáng nǚshì jìcún xínglixiāng liǎng gè, méiyǒu guìzhòng 1606 号 房间 王 女士寄存行李箱 两 个，没有 贵重 wùpǐn. Qǐng zài wǎnshang 9 diǎn yǐqián lái qǔ xíngli. 物品。请在 晚上 9点 以前来取行李。	
kèrén: 客人：	Hǎo de, xièxie! 好 的，谢谢！	
qiántái jiēdàiyuán: 前台 接待员：	Bú kèqi! 不客气！	

译文 yìwén Text in English

Guest: Hello! I'd like to deposit my luggage.

Receptionist: How many pieces of luggage do you want to deposit?

Guest: Two suitcases.

Receptionist: Are there any valuables in your suitcases?

Guest: No.

Receptionist: May I have your name and room number?

Guest: Wang Yi, Room 1606.

Receptionist: When will you pick them up?

Guest: Around 5 o'clock this afternoon.

Receptionist: Ms. Wang in Room 1606 deposits two suitcases. There are no valuables in them. Please come and pick up your suitcases before 9 p.m.

Guest: OK, thanks!

Receptionist: You're welcome!

普通词语 pǔtōng cíyǔ General Vocabulary 🎧 05-05

1.	件	jiàn	m.	a measure word for countable nouns
2.	贵重	guìzhòng	adj.	valuable
3.	物品	wùpǐn	n.	goods
4.	来	lái	v.	come
5.	左右	zuǒyòu	n.	used in a numeral to indicate approximation
6.	以前	yǐqián	n.	previous time

专业词语 zhuānyè cíyǔ Specialized Vocabulary 🎧 05-06

行李箱	xínglixiāng	n.	suitcase

三、视听说 shì-tīng-shuō Viewing, Listening and Speaking

1. 观看礼宾员为客人提供行李服务的视频，根据听到的内容选择正确选项，两人一组，模拟对话。
Watch the video about the concierge providing luggage service for the guest. Choose the right answers based on what you hear, and simulate the conversation in pairs.

sòng xíngli dào kèrén fángjiān
送 行李 到 客人 房间
Sending Luggage to the Guest's Room

lǐbīnyuán: Xiàwǔ hǎo, xiānsheng. Wǒ jiāng dài nín qù fángjiān,
礼宾员：下午 好，先生。我 将 带 您 去 房间， ① ？

kèrén: Shìde.
客人：是的。

lǐbīnyuán:
礼宾员： ② ？

kèrén: Méiyǒu.
客人：没有。

lǐbīnyuán: (náshàng kèrén de xíngli) Zhèbiān qǐng. (Zài děng diàntī) Xiānsheng,
礼宾员：（拿上 客人的 行李）这边 请。（在 等 电梯）先生， ③ 。

kèrén: Gěi nǐ.
客人：给你。

lǐbīnyuán: Nín de fángjiān dào le, (dǎkāi fángmén bìng qǔ diàn kāi dēng) nín xiān qǐng, wǒ kěyǐ bǎ nín de xíngli
礼宾员：您的 房间 到了，（打开 房门 并 取电 开灯）您 先 请，我 可以 把 您的 行李
fàngzài zhèlǐ ma?
放在这里吗？

kèrén:	Kěyǐ.	
客人：	可以。	
lǐbīnyuán:	Qǐngwèn hái yǒu shénme kěyǐ bāng nín ma?	
礼宾员：	请问还有什么可以帮您吗？	
kèrén:	Méiyǒu le, jiù zhèxiē.	
客人：	没有了，就这些。	
lǐbīnyuán:		
礼宾员：	④ 。	
kèrén:	Hǎo de, xièxie nǐ!	
客人：	好的，谢谢你！	

A. kěyǐ jièyòng nín de fángkǎ shuā diàntī ma
可以借用您的房卡刷电梯吗
May I swipe your card to take the elevator?

B. zhè shì nín de liǎng gè xínglixiāng ma
这是您的两个行李箱吗
Are these your two suitcases?

C. qǐngwèn nín de xíngli lǐ yǒu guìzhòng wùpǐn huò yì suì wùpǐn ma
请问您的行李里有贵重物品或易碎物品吗
Are there any valuables or fragile items in your luggage?

D. rúguǒ nín yǒu rènhé yíwèn, kěyǐ liánxì wǒmen
如果您有任何疑问，可以联系我们
If you have any questions, please contact us.

2. 说一说　Let's talk.

练习说一说礼宾员为客人搬运行李的步骤。

Talk about the steps of luggage service provided by the concierge.

四、学以致用　xuéyǐzhìyòng　Practicing What You Have Learnt

观看礼宾员提供行李服务的视频，将下列流程进行排序。
Watch the video about the concierge providing luggage service, and arrange the following processes in order.

zhù kèrén rùzhù yúkuài
A. 祝客人入住愉快
Wish the guest a pleasant stay

xíngliyuán qiāo mén bìng biǎomíng zìjǐ de shēnfèn
B. 行李员敲门并表明自己的身份
The porter knocks at the door and introduces himself

xíngliyuán náhuí xínglipái
C. 行李员拿回行李牌
The porter takes back the luggage tag

kèrén héduì xíngli, bìng xiàng xíngliyuán biǎoshì gǎnxiè
D. 客人核对行李，并向行李员表示感谢
The guest checks the luggage and expresses his/her gratitude to the porter

kèrén dǎkāi fángmén
E. 客人打开房门
The guest opens the door

□ ⇒ □ ⇒ □ ⇒ □ ⇒ □ ⇒ □

五、小知识　xiǎo zhīshi　Tips

Jìcún xíngli xiǎo zhīshi
寄存行李小知识

Tōngcháng qíngkuàng xià, jiǔdiàn kěyǐ wèi rùzhù kèrén tígōng miǎnfèi jìcún xíngli fúwù.
通常情况下，酒店可以为入住客人提供免费寄存行李服务。

Dànshì zhùyì búyào zài jìcún de xíngli zhōng fàngzhì guìzhòng wùpǐn. Zài bànlǐ xíngli jìcún
但是注意不要在寄存的行李中放置贵重物品。在办理行李寄存

shí yào tíqián gàozhī jiǔdiàn qǔ xíngli de shíjiān, rúguǒ kèrén wǎn guī, zé yào diànhuà liánxì.
时要提前告知酒店取行李的时间，如果客人晚归，则要电话联系。

Rúguǒ shàngwǔ dàodá jiǔdiàn, bù xiǎng duō jiāo yì tiān de fángfèi, kěyǐ yǔ jiǔdiàn shāngliang xiān
如果上午到达酒店，不想多交一天的房费，可以与酒店商量先

cúnfàng xíngli, xiàwǔ zài bànlǐ rùzhù.
存放行李，下午再办理入住。

Tips for Depositing Luggage

The hotel usually provides free luggage deposit service for a guest who has checked in. But note that do not leave valuables in the luggage deposited. Please inform the hotel in advance when you will collect your luggage. If you come back late, you should call the hotel. If you arrive at the hotel in the morning and don't want to pay for an extra day, you can discuss with the hotel to deposit your luggage first and then check in in the afternoon.

第二部分 Part 2
汉字 Chinese Characters

一、汉字知识 Hànzì zhīshi Knowledge about Chinese Characters

1. 汉字的笔画（5） Strokes of Chinese characters (5)

笔画 Strokes	名称 Names	例字 Examples
丶	斜钩 xiégōu	我
乚	卧钩 wògōu	心
𠃍	横折钩 héngzhégōu	问
乙	横折弯钩 héngzhéwāngōu	几

2. 汉字的结构（1） Structures of Chinese characters (1)

结构类型 Structure type	例字 Examples	结构图示 Illustration
独体结构 Independent structure	生 不	□

二、汉字认读与书写　Hànzì rèndú yǔ shūxiě　The Recognition and Writing of Chinese Characters

认读下列词语，并试着读写构成词语的汉字。
Recognize the following words, and try to read and write the Chinese characters forming these words.

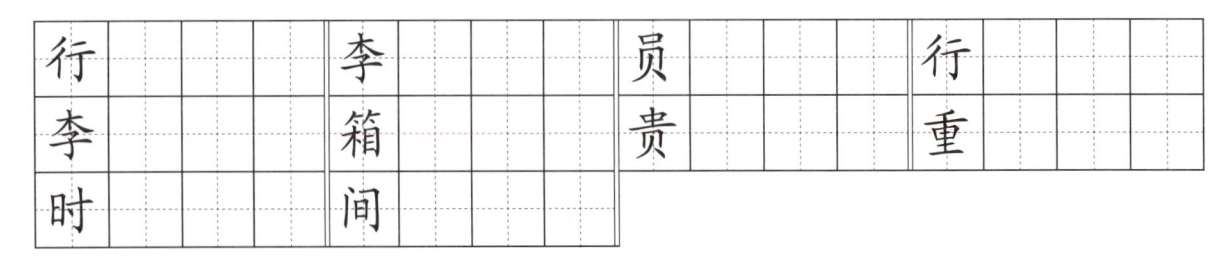

行李员　　行李箱　　贵重　　时间

行			李			员		行	
李			箱			贵		重	
时			间						

第三部分　Part 3　日常用语　Daily Expressions

① 我要两张 11 号到上海的火车票。Wǒ yào liǎng zhāng 11 hào dào Shànghǎi de huǒchēpiào.
I need two train tickets to Shanghai on the 11th.

② 我的护照和钱包都丢了。Wǒ de hùzhào hé qiánbāo dōu diū le. I've lost my passport and wallet.

③ 还可以便宜一些吗？ Hái kěyǐ piányi yìxiē ma? Can you make it cheaper?

第四部分　Part 4　单元实训　Unit Practical Training

模拟行李服务
Simulated Luggage Service

实训目的 Training purpose

通过本次实训，了解并熟练掌握酒店办理行李服务的步骤流程和服务用语。
Through the training, students will get to know and master proficiently the steps of luggage service in a hotel and the service expressions used during the process.

实训组织 Training organization

每组 2～3 人
2-3 students in each group

实训内容 Training content

某酒店客人想要办理行李服务。
A guest in a hotel needs luggage service.

实训步骤 Training steps

❶ 教师将实训教室分成若干个虚拟的酒店前台。
The teacher divides the classroom into several mimetic hotel receptions.

❷ 将参加实训的学员分成若干小组，每组 2～3 人。
Divide the students into groups of 2-3.

❸ 带领学员模拟提供行李服务的情景，过程中给予学员适当帮助。
Guide the students to simulate luggage service and provide them with appropriate help during the process.

❹ 小组成员轮流扮演客人和前台接待员，练习并表演对话。
The group members take turns to play guests and receptionists, practicing and acting out the dialogs.

❺ 教师总结评价，实训结束。
The teacher makes a summary and evaluation, and ends the training.

第五部分　Part 5　单元小结 Unit Summary

词语 cíyǔ Vocabulary

普通词语　General Vocabulary

1.	其他	qítā	pron.	other
2.	过	guò	v.	spend (time), pass (time)
3.	随后	suíhòu	adv.	then
4.	件	jiàn	m.	a measure word for countable nouns
5.	贵重	guìzhòng	adj.	valuable
6.	物品	wùpǐn	n.	goods
7.	来	lái	v.	come
8.	左右	zuǒyòu	n.	used in a numeral to indicate approximation
9.	以前	yǐqián	n.	previous time

专业词语　Specialized Vocabulary

1.	行李员	xínglǐyuán	n.	porter
2.	行李箱	xínglǐxiāng	n.	suitcase

句子 jùzi Sentences

1. 麻烦您填写行李牌。
2. 随后我们会安排行李员将您的行李送到您的房间。
3. 请问您要寄存几件行李？
4. 请问您的行李箱中有贵重物品吗？
5. 请问您什么时候来取？

6 Wǎnglào fúwù
网络服务
Internet Service

wǎngluò fúwù
网络 服务
Internet Service

jiǔdiàn fángjiān wǎngluò liánjiē zhǐnán
酒店房间 网络 连接指南
Guide to the hotel room web connection

wǎngluò liánjiē biāoshí
网络 连接 标识
Web connection signboard

wǎngluò liánjiē jièmiàn
网络 连接 界面
Web connection interface

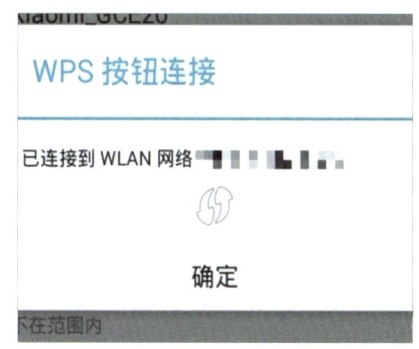

liánjiē chénggōng biāoshí
连接 成功 标识
Successful connection sign

65

题解　Introduction

1. 学习内容：酒店网络服务的流程和服务用语。
   Learning content: The process and service expressions for Internet service in a hotel.
2. 知识目标：掌握网络服务相关的核心词语，学习汉字的笔画"ɿ""ʒ"和品字形结构，学写本单元相关汉字。
   Knowledge objectives: To master the core vocabulary related to Internet service, learn the strokes "ɿ", "ʒ" and 品-shaped structure of Chinese characters, and write the characters related to this unit.
3. 技能目标：能帮助客人连接酒店网络。
   Skill objective: To be able to help a guest connect to hotel Wi-Fi.

第一部分　Part 1

课文　Texts

一、热身　rèshēn　Warm-up

1. 给词语选择对应的图片。　Choose the corresponding pictures for the words.

A

B

C

D

❶ WLAN 连接 _____
　WLAN　liánjiē
　WLAN connection

❷ 路由器 _____
　lùyóuqì
　router

❸ 无线 网络 _____
　wúxiàn wǎngluò
　Wi-Fi

❹ 手机 _____
　shǒujī
　mobile phone

66

2. 观看视频，根据视频内容选择正确选项。
Watch the video, and choose the right answers based on the video.

xúnwèn qiántái wǎngluò mìmǎ
① 询问 前台 网络 密码 _____
Asking the receptionist for the network password

qǐng gōngzuò rényuán bāngmáng liánjiē wúxiàn wǎngluò
② 请 工作 人员 帮忙 连接 无线 网络 _____
Asking the staff to help connect to hotel Wi-Fi

fángjiān wǎngluò bù wěndìng, diànhuà zīxún qiántái
③ 房间 网络 不稳定，电话 咨询 前台 _____
Calling the receptionist because of the unstable Internet connection of the room

xúnwèn qiántái rúhé liánjiē jiǔdiàn wúxiàn wǎngluò
④ 询问 前台 如何 连接 酒店 无线 网络 _____
Consulting the receptionist how to connect to hotel Wi-Fi

A. ▶ B. ▶ C. ▶ D. ▶

二、课文 kèwén Texts

A 06-01

客人: 你好，我想知道在我的房间能不能接入无线网络？

前台服务员: 可以的。

客人: 能告诉我怎么连接笔记本电脑吗？

前台服务员: 您能在您的电脑上找到网络图标吗？它通常在任务栏的右边。

客人: 好的。

前台服务员: 现在请点击网络图标，看可用网络列表，您应该能看到我们酒店的无线网络名称。

客人: 好的，我看到了。

前台服务员: 现在点击连接按钮，密码是房间号码。

客人: 太棒了，我能上网了！

前台服务员: 请问还有什么需要帮忙的吗？

客人: 不用了，谢谢。

译文 yìwén Text in English

Guest: Hello! I wonder if my room has Wi-Fi.

Receptionist: Yes, it has.

Guest: Can you tell me how to connect my laptop to it?

Receptionist: Can you find the network icon on the screen of your computer? It is usually on the right side of the taskbar.

Guest: Yes.

网络服务 6
Internet Service

Receptionist: Now please click on the network icon to see the list of available networks and you should be able to find our hotel Wi-Fi in it.
Guest: Yes, I see it.
Receptionist: Now click the button to connect and the password is your room number.
Guest: Great! I have access to the Internet now.
Receptionist: Is there anything else I can do for you?
Guest: No, thank you.

普通词语 pǔtōng cíyǔ General Vocabulary 06-02

1.	接入	jiērù	phr.	have access to
2.	连接	liánjiē	v.	connect
3.	通常	tōngcháng	adj.	usually
4.	右边	yòubian	n.	right side
	右	yòu	n.	right
5.	可用	kě yòng	phr.	available
	用	yòng	v.	use
6.	列表	lièbiǎo	n.	list
7.	应该	yīnggāi	v.	ought to
8.	名称	míngchēng	n.	name
9.	密码	mìmǎ	n.	password
10.	太	tài	adv.	too, excessively
11.	棒	bàng	adj.	great, wonderful
12.	上网	shàng//wǎng	v.	surf the Internet
13.	帮忙	bāng//máng	v.	help

专业词语 zhuānyè cíyǔ Specialized Vocabulary 06-03

1.	无线	wúxiàn	adj.	wireless
2.	笔记本电脑	bǐjìběn diànnǎo	phr.	laptop
	电脑	diànnǎo	n.	computer
3.	图标	túbiāo	n.	icon
4.	任务栏	rènwulán	n.	taskbar
5.	点击	diǎnjī	v.	click
6.	按钮	ànniǔ	n.	button

69

B

客人: 你好，我想知道酒店里面有没有无线网络？

前台接待员: 有的，酒店所有地方都有免费无线网，没有密码，您只需要使用您的名字和房间号来登录就可以了。

客人: 好的，我试一下。不知道为什么我的手机上不了网。

前台接待员: 我能看一下您的手机吗？

客人: 当然。

前台接待员: 我能更改一下您手机的设置吗？

客人: 为什么？

前台接待员: 您的手机设置了不允许连接公共无线网。

客人: 好的。

前台接待员: 已经改好了，您再试一下。

客人: 可以了，谢谢。

译文 yìwén Text in English

Guest: Hello! I'd like to know if the hotel has Wi-Fi.

Receptionist: Yes, free Wi-Fi is available everywhere in the hotel, and no password is required. You just need to log in using your name and room number.

Guest: OK, let me try. I don't know why my mobile phone can't be connected to the Wi-Fi.

Receptionist: Can I have a look at your phone?

Guest: Of course.

Receptionist: Can I change the settings on your phone?

Guest: Why?

Receptionist: It is set that your mobile phone is not allowed to connect to public Wi-Fi.

Guest: OK.
Receptionist: It has been changed. Would you try it again?
Guest: It's connected. Thank you.

普通词语 pǔtōng cíyǔ General Vocabulary 🎧 06-05

1.	里面	lǐmiàn	n.	inside
2.	所有	suǒyǒu	adj.	all
3.	地方	dìfang	n.	place
4.	免费	miǎn//fèi	v.	be free (of charge)
5.	使用	shǐyòng	v.	use
6.	试	shì	v.	try
7.	为什么	wèi shénme	phr.	why
8.	手机	shǒujī	n.	mobile phone
9.	更改	gēnggǎi	v.	change
	改	gǎi	v.	change
10.	允许	yǔnxǔ	v.	allow
11.	公共	gōnggòng	adj.	public
12.	再	zài	adv.	again

专业词语 zhuānyè cíyǔ Specialized Vocabulary 🎧 06-06

	设置	shèzhì	v.	set, set up

三、视听说 shì-tīng-shuō Viewing, Listening and Speaking

1. 观看前台接待员帮客人接入无线网络的视频，根据听到的内容选择正确选项，两人一组，模拟对话。
Watch the video about the receptionist helping the guest connect to Wi-Fi. Choose the right answers based on what you hear and simulate a conversation in pairs.

wǎngluò liánjiē gùzhàng jiějué
网络 连接 故障 解决
Network Connection Troubleshooting

kèrén: Nǐ hǎo, wǒ shì 1606 fángjiān de kèrén, qǐngwèn shì shénme yuányīn ne?
客人：你好，我是1606房间的客人，① ，请问 是什么 原因 呢？

qiántái jiēdàiyuán: Wúxiàn wǎngluò míngchēng shì Jīnlíng Jiǔdiàn,
前台 接待员：无线 网络 名称 是金陵酒店，② 。

kèrén: Wǒ zài shì yí cì,
客人：我再试一次，③ 。

qiántái jiēdàiyuán: Hǎo de, qǐngwèn hái yǒu shénme xūyào bāngmáng de ma?
前台 接待员：好的，请问还有 什么需要 帮忙 的吗？

kèrén: Méiyǒu le, xièxie!
客人：没有了，谢谢！

qiántái jiēdàiyuán: Bú kèqi,
前台 接待员：不客气，④ ！

mìmǎ shì nín de fángjiānhào 1606
A. 密码是您的房间号1606
The password is your room number 1606

xiànzài liánjiē shàng le
B. 现在连接 上 了
Now it's connected

zhù nín rùzhù yúkuài
C. 祝 您入住 愉快
Enjoy your stay

wǒ de shǒujī méi bànfǎ liánjiē jiǔdiàn de wúxiàn wǎngluò
D. 我的手机没 办法连接酒店的无线 网络
I can't connect my phone to the hotel Wi-Fi

2. 说一说 Let's talk.

练习说一说连接酒店无线网络的步骤。

Talk about the steps of connecting to the hotel Wi-Fi.

6 网络服务 Internet Service

四、学以致用 xuéyǐzhìyòng Practicing What You Have Learnt

观看介绍连接无线网络的视频，将下列操作流程进行排序。
Watch the video introducing how to connect to Wi-Fi and arrange the following processes in order.

① liánjiē chénggōng 连接 成功 Connecting successfully

② xúnzhǎo jiǔdiàn míngchēng 寻找 酒店 名称 Finding the hotel's name

③ dǎkāi shǒujī 打开 手机 Turning on the mobile phone

④ zhǎodào shèzhì 找到 设置 Finding the Settings

⑤ diǎnjī liánjiē 点击 连接 Clicking Connect

⑥ shūrù mìmǎ 输入 密码 Entering the password

⑦ xuǎnzé WLAN 选择 WLAN Choosing WLAN

☐ → ☐ → ☐ → ☐ → ☐ → ☐ → ☐

五、小知识 xiǎo zhīshi Tips

Jiǔdiàn wǎngluò fúwù
酒店 网络 服务

Rújīn jiǔdiàn dōu wèi zhù diàn kèrén tígōng miǎnfèi, wěndìng hé ānquán de wǎngluò fúwù.
如今酒店 都 为 住 店客人 提供 免费、稳定和安全的网络 服务。

Jiǔdiàn dàtáng, kèfáng, huìyìshì de yǒuxiàn / wúxiàn wǎngluò nénggòu chōngfèn mǎnzú kèrén
酒店大堂、客房、会议室的有线/无线网络 能够 充分 满足 客人

de wǎngluò jiērù xūqiú, tíshēng zhùkè duì jiǔdiàn fúwù de zhěngtǐ mǎnyìdù. Zài hùliánwǎng
的网络接入需求，提升 住客对酒店服务的整体满意度。在 互联网

gāosù fāzhǎn de shídài, tígōng biànlì de wǎngluò yǐjīng chéngwéi jiǔdiàn de jīchǔ fúwù.
高速发展的时代，提供 便利的网络 已经 成为 酒店的基础服务。

Hotel Wi-Fi Service

Nowadays, most hotels provide free, stable and safe Wi-Fi for their guests. The Internet service in the hotel lobby, guest rooms and conference rooms can fully meet the guests' needs to access the

73

Internet and improve their overall satisfaction with the hotel service. In the era characterized by rapid development of the Internet, providing convenient access to the Internet has become a fundamental service in a hotel.

第二部分 Part 2 汉字 Chinese Characters

一、汉字知识　Hànzì zhīshi　Knowledge about Chinese Characters

1. 汉字的笔画（6） Strokes of Chinese characters (6)

笔画 Strokes	名称 Names	例字 Examples
ㄋ	横撇弯钩 héngpiěwāngōu	部
ㄋ	横折折折钩 héngzhézhézhégōu	奶

2. 汉字的结构（2） Structures of Chinese characters (2)

结构类型 Structure type	例字 Example	结构图示 Illustration
品字形结构 品-shaped structure	品	⊞

二、汉字认读与书写　Hànzì rèndú yǔ shūxiě　The Recognition and Writing of Chinese Characters

认读下列词语，并试着读写构成词语的汉字。
Recognize the following words, and try to read and write the Chinese characters forming these words.

电脑　手机　无线　密码

| 电 | | 脑 | | 手 | | 机 |
| 无 | | 线 | | 密 | | 码 |

第三部分　Part 3　日常用语 Daily Expressions

❶ 请原谅。Qǐng yuánliàng. Sorry.
❷ 不好意思，麻烦你…… Bù hǎoyìsi, máfan nǐ… Excuse me, could you please...
❸ 我前几天感冒了。Wǒ qián jǐ tiān gǎnmào le. I had a cold several days ago.

第四部分　Part 4　单元实训 Unit Practical Training

模拟酒店无线网络服务
Simulated Hotel Wi-Fi Service

实训目的 Training purpose
通过本次实训，了解并熟练掌握酒店网络连接的步骤流程和服务用语。

Through the training, students will get to know and master proficiently the steps of the Wi-Fi connection of a hotel and the service expressions used during the process.

实训组织 Training organization
每组 2～3 人

2-3 students in each group

实训内容 Training content
某酒店客人无法连接酒店免费 Wi-Fi，前台经过了解后，成功帮该客人接入网络。

A guest cannot connect to hotel free Wi-Fi. After learning the situation, the receptionist helps him/her get connected to the Internet.

实训步骤 Training steps
❶ 教师将实训教室分成若干个虚拟的酒店前台。

　 The teacher divides the classroom into several mimetic hotel receptions.
❷ 将参加实训的学员分成若干小组，每组 2～3 人。

　 Divide the students into groups of 2-3.
❸ 带领学员模拟为客人提供酒店网络服务的对话，过程中给予学员适当帮助。

　 Guide the students to make simulated conversations about helping guests gain access to the Internet in a hotel, and provide them with appropriate assistance during the process.
❹ 小组成员轮流扮演客人和前台接待员，练习并表演对话。

　 The group members take turns to play guests and receptionists, practicing and acting out the dialogs.
❺ 教师总结评价，实训结束。

　 The teacher makes a summary and evaluation, and ends the training.

第五部分　Part 5　单元小结　Unit Summary

词语 cíyǔ　Vocabulary

普通词语　General Vocabulary

1.	接入	jiērù	phr.	have access to
2.	连接	liánjiē	v.	connect
3.	通常	tōngcháng	adj.	usually
4.	右边	yòubian	n.	right side
	右	yòu	n.	right
5.	可用	kě yòng	phr.	available
	用	yòng	v.	use
6.	列表	lièbiǎo	n.	list
7.	应该	yīnggāi	v.	ought to
8.	名称	míngchēng	n.	name
9.	密码	mìmǎ	n.	password
10.	太	tài	adv.	too, excessively
11.	棒	bàng	adj.	great, wonderful
12.	上网	shàng//wǎng	v.	surf the Internet
13.	帮忙	bāng//máng	v.	help
14.	里面	lǐmiàn	n.	inside
15.	所有	suǒyǒu	adj.	all
16.	地方	dìfang	n.	place
17.	免费	miǎn//fèi	v.	be free (of charge)
18.	使用	shǐyòng	v.	use
19.	试	shì	v.	try
20.	为什么	wèi shénme	phr.	why
21.	手机	shǒujī	n.	mobile phone
22.	更改	gēnggǎi	v.	change
	改	gǎi	v.	change
23.	允许	yǔnxǔ	v.	allow
24.	公共	gōnggòng	adj.	public
25.	再	zài	adv.	again

网络服务 6
Internet Service

专业词语 Specialized Vocabulary

1.	无线	wúxiàn	adj.	wireless
2.	笔记本电脑	bǐjìběn diànnǎo	phr.	laptop
	电脑	diànnǎo	n.	computer
3.	图标	túbiāo	n.	icon
4.	任务栏	rènwulán	n.	taskbar
5.	点击	diǎnjī	v.	click
6.	按钮	ànniǔ	n.	button
7.	设置	shèzhì	v.	set, set up

cíyǔ 词语 Vocabulary

jùzi 句子 Sentences

1. 请点击网络图标，看可用网络列表。
2. 您应该能看到我们酒店的网络名称。
3. 现在点击连接按钮，密码是房间号码。
4. 酒店里所有地方都有免费无线网。
5. 我能更改一下您手机的设置吗？

7

Fáng nèi yòngcān fúwù
房内用餐服务
In-Room Dining Service

fáng nèi yòngcān fúwù nèiróng
房内用餐服务内容
In-Room Dining Service Includes:

yǐnliào fúwù: lěngyǐn, rèyǐn, jiǔlèi děng
饮料服务：冷饮、热饮、酒类等
Beverage service: cold drinks, hot drinks, and wine, etc.

shípǐn fúwù: zǎocān, wǔcān, wǎncān, diǎnxin děng
食品服务：早餐、午餐、晚餐、点心等
Food service: breakfast, lunch, supper and snacks, etc.

tèbié fúwù: VIP zhùkè de tèshū sòngcān fúwù
特别服务：VIP 住客的特殊送餐服务
Special service: special meal delivery for designated VIP guests

fáng nèi yòngcān fúwù liúchéng
房内用餐服务流程
In-Room Dining Service Process

jìlù kèrén fánghào jí yòngcān xūqiú
记录客人房号及用餐需求
Recording the guest's room number and his/her dining needs

dìngdān tíjiāo chúfáng
订单提交厨房
Submitting the order to the kitchen

shōu cān
收餐
Tidying up after dinner

wènqīng fùkuǎn fāngshì
问清付款方式
Inquiring about the payment method

sòng cān
送餐
Delivering meals

jiézhàng
结账 
Settling accounts

79

> **题解　Introduction**
>
> 1. 学习内容：酒店客房订餐和送餐服务的流程和服务用语。
>   Learning content: The process and service expressions for in-room dining and delivery service in a hotel.
> 2. 知识目标：掌握房内用餐相关的核心词语，学习汉字的笔画"㇆""乀"和上下结构、上中下结构，学写本单元相关汉字。
>   Knowledge objectives: To master the core vocabulary related to in-room dining, learn the strokes "㇆", "乀", top-bottom structure and top-middle-bottom structure of Chinese characters, and write the characters related to this unit.
> 3. 技能目标：能正确应对客人对房内用餐的需求。
>   Skill objective: To be able to respond to a guest's requirement for in-room dining.

第一部分　Part 1

课文　Texts

一、热身　rèshēn　Warm-up

1. 给词语选择对应的图片。　Choose the corresponding pictures for the words.

A

B

C

D

　　sòng cān
① 送 餐＿＿＿＿＿＿＿＿
　　meal delivery

　　fáng nèi yòngcān
② 房 内 用餐＿＿＿＿＿＿＿＿
　　in-room dining

　　niúpái
③ 牛排＿＿＿＿＿＿＿＿
　　steak

　　hóngjiǔ
④ 红酒＿＿＿＿＿＿＿＿
　　red wine

80

房内用餐服务 7
In-Room Dining Service

2. 观看介绍酒店各种服务的视频，根据视频内容选择正确选项。
Watch the video introducing various service of a hotel. Choose the right answers based on the video.

❶ yòngcān fúwù
用餐服务_____
dining service

❷ zǒngjī fúwù
总机服务_____
operator service

❸ sòng cān fúwù
送餐服务_____
meal delivery service

❹ kèfáng fúwù
客房服务_____
room service

A. ▶　　B. ▶　　C. ▶　　D. ▶

二、课文　kèwén　Texts

A 　07-01

zǒngjīyuán: Shàngwǔ hǎo, qǐngwèn yǒu shénme néng wèi nín xiàoláo?
总机员：上午好，请问有什么能为您效劳？

kèrén: Nín hǎo, wǒ xiǎng zài fángjiān yòng wǔcān, xūyào sòng cān fúwù.
客人：您好，我想在房间用午餐，需要送餐服务。

zǒngjīyuán: Wǒmen yǒu liǎng zhǒng tàocān gōng nín xuǎnzé, niúròumiàn tàocān hé jīròufàn tàocān. Nín xǐhuan nǎ zhǒng?
总机员：我们有两种套餐供您选择，牛肉面套餐和鸡肉饭套餐。您喜欢哪种？

kèrén: 客人：	Wǒ xiǎng diǎn niúròumiàn tàocān. 我想点牛肉面套餐。	
zǒngjīyuán: 总机员：	Nín xiǎng hē shénme, chá, kāfēi, háishi hóngjiǔ? 您想喝什么，茶、咖啡，还是红酒？	
kèrén: 客人：	Lái yì hú lǜchá. 来一壶绿茶。	
zǒngjīyuán: 总机员：	Gēn nín quèrèn yíxià, yí fèn niúròumiàn tàocān, yì hú lǜchá. 跟您确认一下，一份牛肉面套餐，一壶绿茶。	
kèrén: 客人：	Bàoqiàn, wǒmen shì liǎng rén yòngcān, liǎng fèn niúròumiàn, yì hú lǜchá. Qǐng 抱歉，我们是两人用餐，两份牛肉面，一壶绿茶。请 zhōngwǔ 11 diǎn 30 sòng cān. 中午11点30送餐。	
zǒngjīyuán: 总机员：	Hǎode, mǎshàng wèi nín zhǔnbèi, sòngcānyuán huì ànshí sòngdào. 好的，马上为您准备，送餐员会按时送到。	
kèrén: 客人：	Xièxie. 谢谢。	

译文 yìwén Text in English

Operator: Good morning! What can I do for you?

Guest: Hello! I'd like to have lunch in my room. I need meal delivery service.

Operator: We have two combos for you: beef noodles combo and chicken rice combo. Which one do you prefer?

Guest: I prefer beef noodles combo.

Operator: What would you like to drink, tea, coffee or red wine?

Guest: A pot of green tea, please.

Operator: Just to confirm, a beef noodles combo and a pot of green tea.

Guest: Sorry, it's for two of us, so we need two beef noodles combos and a pot of green tea. Please deliver the meal at 11:30 a.m.

Operator: All right. We'll get it ready for you right away. The delivery man will deliver it on time.

Guest: Thank you.

普通词语 pǔtōng cíyǔ General Vocabulary　　🎧 07-02

1.	效劳	xiào//láo	v.	work for
2.	种	zhǒng	m.	kind, type
3.	供	gōng	v.	provide sth. for (the use or convenience of)
4.	选择	xuǎnzé	v./n.	choose; choice

82

5.	牛肉面	niúròumiàn	phr.	beef noodles
6.	鸡肉饭	jīròufàn	phr.	chicken rice
7.	点	diǎn	v.	order, ask for sth. to eat or drink in a restaurant, bar, etc.
8.	喝	hē	v.	drink
9.	茶	chá	n.	tea
10.	咖啡	kāfēi	n.	coffee
11.	红酒	hóngjiǔ	n.	red wine
12.	壶	hú	m.	pot
13.	绿茶	lǜchá	n.	green tea
14.	份	fèn	m.	share, portion
15.	按时	ànshí	adv.	on time

专业词语 zhuānyè cíyǔ Specialized Vocabulary   07-03

1.	送餐	sòng cān	phr.	deliver meals
2.	套餐	tàocān	n.	combo, set meal
3.	送餐员	sòngcānyuán	n.	delivery man

B 07-04

sòngcānyuán:
送餐员: Nín hǎo, sòngcānyuán.
您好，送餐员。

kèrén:
客人: Nín hǎo, qǐng jìn.
您好，请进。

sòngcānyuán:
送餐员: Zhè shì nín diǎn de cān, gěi nín fàng zài zhèlǐ kěyǐ ma?
这是您点的餐，给您放在这里可以吗？

kèrén:
客人: Méiyǒu wèntí, xīnkǔ nǐ le.
没有问题，辛苦你了。

sòngcānyuán:
送餐员: Lǜchá xūyào xiànzài gěi nín dàoshang ma?
绿茶需要现在给您倒上吗？

kèrén:
客人: Wǒ zìjǐ lái jiù kěyǐ le.
我自己来就可以了。

sòngcānyuán:
送餐员: Nín shì xiǎng fù xiànjīn háishi guàzhàng?
您是想付现金还是挂账？

kèrén: Guàzhàng ba, tuì fáng de shíhou wǒ yìqǐ jiézhàng.
客人：挂账 吧，退 房 的 时候 我 一起 结账。

sòngcānyuán: Hǎo de, qǐng bǎ nín de xìngmíng hé fánghào qiān zài zhàngdān shàng. Xièxie, zhù
送餐员：好的，请 把 您 的 姓名 和 房号 签 在 账单 上。谢谢，祝

nín yòngcān yúkuài!
您 用餐 愉快！

译文 yìwén Text in English

Delivery man: Hello, meal delivery for you.

Guest: Hello, come in, please.

Delivery man: This is the meal you ordered. May I put it here?

Guest: No problem. Thank you very much.

Delivery man: Would you like the green tea to be served now?

Guest: I'd like to help myself to it.

Delivery man: Would you like to pay by cash or city ledger?

Guest: By city ledger. I'll pay the bill when I check out.

Delivery man: All right. Please sign your name and room number on the bill. Thank you. Enjoy your meal!

普通词语 pǔtōng cíyǔ General Vocabulary 🎧 07-05

1.	请进	qǐng jìn	phr.	Please come in.
	进	jìn	v.	enter
2.	放	fàng	v.	put
3.	辛苦	xīnkǔ	adj./v.	hard; work laboriously
4.	倒	dào	v.	pour
5.	自己	zìjǐ	pron.	oneself
6.	一起	yìqǐ	adv./n.	together; being in the same place
7.	结账	jié//zhàng	v.	check out

专业词语 zhuānyè cíyǔ Specialized Vocabulary 🎧 07-06

	挂账	guà//zhàng	v.	pay by city ledger

三、视听说　shì-tīng-shuō　Viewing, Listening and Speaking

1. 观看总机员为客人预订房内用餐服务的视频，将下列服务流程进行排序。
Watch the video about the telephone operator booking an in-room dining service for the guest and arrange the following service processes in order.

　　　　　　　　qiántái　jiēshòu　dìngcān
　　　　　　　　前台 接受 订餐
　　　　　　　　Taking Orders by the Receptionist

querèn yòngcān rénshù
❶ 确认 用餐 人数 Confirming the number of diners

wènhòuyǔ
❷ 问候语 Greetings

xúnwèn fúwù nèiróng
❸ 询问 服务 内容 Inquiring about the service included

querèn sòng cānshíjiān
❹ 确认 送 餐时间 Confirming the delivery time

xúnwèn diǎn cān nèiróng
❺ 询问 点 餐 内容 Asking about the food ordered

querèn diǎn cān nèiróng
❻ 确认 点 餐 内容 Confirming the order

☐ ⇒ ☐ ⇒ ☐ ⇒ ☐ ⇒ ☐ ⇒ ☐

2. 说一说　Let's talk.

练习说一说为客人预订房内用餐的操作步骤以及常用服务用语。
Talk about the steps of ordering in-room dining for a guest and the service expressions frequently used during the process.

四、学以致用　xuéyǐzhìyòng　Practicing What You Have Learnt

观看客人预订房内用餐的视频，将下列表格信息填写完整。
Watch the video about the guest booking an in-room meal, and complete the following table.

fángnèi yòngcān fúwù
房内 用餐 服务
In-room Dining Service

fángjiān hàomǎ 房间号码 Room numbers	kèrén xìngmíng 客人 姓名 Names	diǎn cān 点 餐 Food ordered	shùliàng 数量 Numbers	bèizhù 备注 Remarks
	Lù xiānsheng 陆 先生 Mr. Lu	jīròufàn tàocān + lǜchá 鸡肉饭 套餐 + 绿茶 Chicken rice combo + Green tea		
	Lǐ xiǎojiě 李小姐 Ms. Li	niúròumiàn tàocān + kāfēi 牛肉面 套餐 + 咖啡 Beef noodles combo + Coffee		jiā nǎi bù jiā táng 加奶不加糖 Milk without sugar
	Yú xiǎojiě 余小姐 Ms. Yu	niúpái tàocān + hóngjiǔ 牛排 套餐 + 红酒 Steak combo + Red wine		

五、小知识　xiǎo zhīshi　Tips

Fáng nèi yòngcān fúwù
房 内 用餐服务

　　Jiǔdiàn xiāngguān fúwù rényuán yào liǎojiě dàngtiān jiǔdiàn gōngyìng de shípǐn, bìmiǎn
　　酒店 相关 服务人员 要 了解 当天 酒店 供应 的 食品， 避免
chūxiàn kèrén diǎn cān hòu chúfáng wúfǎ zhìzuò de qíngkuàng. Zài jiēshòu kèrén yùdìng shí yào
出现 客人点餐后 厨房 无法 制作 的 情况。 在 接受 客人 预订 时要

xiángxì jìlù kèrén dìngcān xìnxī, bìng quèrèn bāokuò dìngcān kèrén fángjiān hàomǎ, dìngcān
详细记录客人订餐信息，并确认包括订餐客人房间号码、订餐

nèiróng, yòng cān shíjiān, fúwùyuán xìngmíng jí zhàngdān hàomǎ děng xìnxī. Sòng cān zhǔnbèi
内容、用餐时间、服务员姓名及账单号码等信息。送餐准备

guòchéng zhōng yào jiǎnchá bìng dāpèi xiāngyìng de cānjù, sòng cān tú zhōng bìxū shǐyòng cāngài.
过程中要检查并搭配相应的餐具，送餐途中必须使用餐盖。

Notes for in-room Dining Service

The related service staff should be aware of the food provided by the hotel on that day to avoid the situation that the kitchen cannot make food the guest orders. When accepting a guest's reservation, it is important to note and confirm the guest's booking details including the guest's room number, food ordered, time for the meal, the attendant's name, and the number of the bill. When preparing the meal delivery, it is necessary to check and match the corresponding meal box, and the meal cover must be used.

第二部分　Part 2
汉字　Chinese Characters

一、汉字知识　Hànzì zhīshi　Knowledge about Chinese Characters

1. 汉字的笔画（7）Strokes of Chinese characters (7)

笔画 Strokes	名称 Names	例字 Examples
𠃍	竖折折钩 shùzhézhégōu	马
㇃	横斜钩 héngxiégōu	风

2. 汉字的结构（3）Structures of Chinese characters (3)

结构类型 Structure types	例字 Examples	结构图示 Illustrations
上下结构 Top-bottom structure	爸 学	
上中下结构 Top-middle-bottom structure	意	

二、汉字认读与书写　Hànzì rèndú yǔ shūxiě　The Recognition and Writing of Chinese Characters

认读下列词语，并试着读写构成词语的汉字。
Recognize the following words, and try to read and write the Chinese characters forming these words.

茶　　签　　壶　　套餐　　送餐员

茶				签				壶				套			
餐				送				餐				员			

第三部分　Part 3　日常用语　Daily Expressions

① 麻烦你替我请个假。Máfan nǐ tì wǒ qǐng gè jià. Would you please ask for leave for me?
② 我被骗了。Wǒ bèi piàn le. I was cheated.
③ 别着急。Bié zháojí. Don't worry.

第四部分　Part 4　单元实训　Unit Practical Training

模拟房内用餐服务
Simulated in-room Dining Service

实训目的 Training purpose

通过本次实训，了解并掌握酒店房内用餐服务的流程和服务用语。
Through the training, students will get to know and master proficiently the process of in-room dining service in a hotel and the service expressions used during the process.

实训组织 Training organization

每组 2～3 人
2-3 students in each group

实训内容 Training content

某酒店客人需要房内用餐，请记录客人的订餐服务信息，并安排送餐服务。
A guest in a hotel needs to dine in the room. Please note down the information about his/her order, and arrange the meal delivery.

实训步骤 Training steps

① 教师将实训教室分成若干个虚拟的酒店前台和客房。

The teacher divides the classroom into several mimetic hotel receptions and guest rooms.

❷ 将参加实训的学员分成若干小组，每组 2～3 人。
Divide the students into groups of 2-3.

❸ 带领学员模拟酒店房内用餐服务流程，过程中给予学员适当帮助。
Guide the students to simulate the in-room dining service process in a hotel and provide them with appropriate assistance during the process.

❹ 小组成员轮流扮演客人和前台接待员，练习并表演对话。
The group members take turns to play guests and receptionists, practicing and acting out the dialogs.

❺ 教师总结评价，实训结束。
The teacher makes a summary and evaluation, and ends the training.

第五部分　Part 5　单元小结　Unit Summary

词语 Vocabulary

普通词语　General Vocabulary

1.	效劳	xiào//láo	v.	work for
2.	种	zhǒng	m.	kind, type
3.	供	gōng	v.	provide sth. for (the use or convenience of)
4.	选择	xuǎnzé	v./n.	choose; choice
5.	牛肉面	niúròumiàn	phr.	beef noodles
6.	鸡肉饭	jīròufàn	phr.	chicken rice
7.	点	diǎn	v.	order, ask for sth. to eat or drink in a restaurant, bar, etc.
8.	喝	hē	v.	drink
9.	茶	chá	n.	tea
10.	咖啡	kāfēi	n.	coffee
11.	红酒	hóngjiǔ	n.	red wine
12.	壶	hú	m.	pot
13.	绿茶	lǜchá	n.	green tea
14.	份	fèn	m.	share, portion
15.	按时	ànshí	adv.	on time
16.	请进	qǐng jìn	phr.	Please come in.
	进	jìn	v.	enter
17.	放	fàng	v.	put

18.	辛苦	xīnkǔ	adj./v.	hard; work laboriously
19.	倒	dào	v.	pour
20.	自己	zìjǐ	pron.	oneself
21.	一起	yìqǐ	adv./n.	together; being in the same place
22.	结账	jié//zhàng	v.	check out

cíyǔ 词语 Vocabulary

专业词语　Specialized Vocabulary

1.	送餐	sòng cān	phr.	deliver meals
2.	套餐	tàocān	n.	combo, set meal
3.	送餐员	sòngcānyuán	n.	delivery man
4.	挂账	guà//zhàng	v.	pay by city ledger

jùzi 句子 Sentences

1. 我们有两种套餐供您选择，牛肉面套餐和鸡肉饭套餐。您喜欢哪种？
2. 您想喝什么，茶、咖啡还是红酒？
3. 跟您确认一下，一份牛肉面套餐，一壶绿茶。
4. 马上为您准备，送餐员会按时送到。
5. 这是您点的餐，给您放在这里可以吗？
6. 绿茶需要现在给您倒上吗？
7. 您是想付现金还是挂账？
8. 请把您的姓名和房号签在账单上。
9. 祝您用餐愉快！

8 租借物品服务
Zūjiè wùpǐn fúwù
Rental Service

kě zūjiè wùpǐn
可租借物品
Items for Rent

yǔsǎn	chōngdiànqì	zhuǎnjiētóu	diànyùndòu
雨伞	充电器	转接头	电熨斗
Umbrella	Charger	Adapter	Electric iron

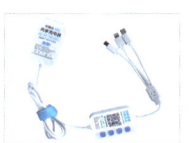

wùpǐn zūjiè fúwù liúchéng
物品租借服务流程
Item Rental Service Process

wènhòu kèrén
问候 客人
Greeting the guest

dēngjì kèrén xìnxī
登记客人信息
Registering the guest's information

shōuhuí zūjiè wùpǐn
收回租借物品
Taking back the rented item

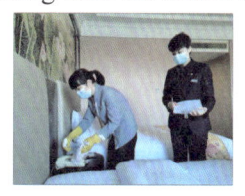

xúnwèn zūjiè wùpǐn
询问租借物品
Inquiring about the rented item

ānpái zūjiè wùpǐn
安排租借物品
Arranging the rented item

题解　Introduction

1. 学习内容：酒店租借物品服务的流程和服务用语。
   Learning content: The process and service expressions for rental service in a hotel.
2. 知识目标：掌握租借物品相关的核心词语，学习汉字的笔画"乚""乁"和左右结构、左中右结构，学写本单元相关汉字。
   Knowledge objectives: To master the core vocabulary related to rental service, learn the strokes "乚", "乁", left-right structure and left-middle-right structure of Chinese characters, and write the characters related to this unit.
3. 技能目标：能为客人提供酒店租借物品服务。
   Skill objective: To be able to provide rental service for a hotel guest.

第一部分　Part 1

课文　Texts

一、热身　rèshēn　Warm-up

1. 给词语选择对应的图片。　Choose the corresponding pictures for the words.

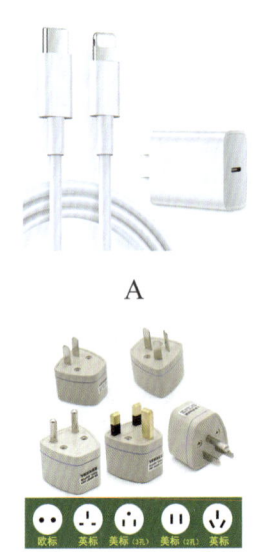

A

B

C

D

① yǔsǎn
雨伞＿＿＿＿＿＿＿
umbrella

② zhuǎnjiētóu
转接头＿＿＿＿＿＿＿
adapter

③ chōngdiànqì
充电器＿＿＿＿＿＿＿
charger

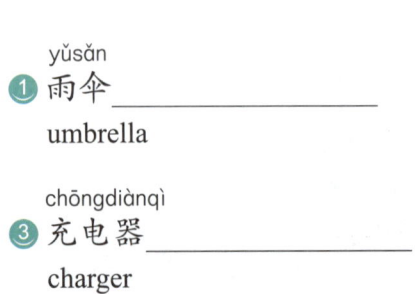

④ shāoshuǐhú
烧水壶＿＿＿＿＿＿＿
kettle

8 租借物品服务
Rental Service

2. 观看介绍酒店租借服务的视频，根据视频内容选择正确选项。
Watch the video introducing the rental service in a hotel. Choose the right answers based on the video.

租借 服务 介绍
zūjiè fúwù jièshào
Introduction to rental service

① Yìbān de jiǔdiàn dōu huì tígōng xiāngyìng de
一般的酒店 都 会 提供 相 应 的 ＿＿＿＿＿＿＿。
A hotel usually provides the corresponding ＿＿＿＿＿＿.

② Rúguǒ xūyào zūjiè wùpǐn, nǐ xūyào dào qiántái jìnxíng　　　　　bànlǐ
如果 需要 租借 物品，你 需要 到 前台 进行 ＿＿＿＿，办理 ＿＿＿＿。
If you need to rent something, you need to go to the receptionist to go through the ＿＿＿＿＿＿ for the ＿＿＿＿＿＿.

A. 租借服务　　　　B. 租借手续　　　　C. 租借登记
　　zūjiè fúwù　　　　　　zūjiè shǒuxù　　　　　zūjiè dēngjì
　　rental service　　　　rental procedure　　　rental registration

二、课文 kèwén Texts

93

A 🎧 08-01

客人: Nín hǎo! wǒ shì 801 fángjiān de Lǐ Míng, wǒ de shǒujī méi diàn le.
客人: 您好！我是801房间的李明，我的手机没电了。

前台 接待员: Xūyào wèi nín tígōng zūjiè fúwù ma?
前台 接待员: 需要为您提供租借服务吗？

客人: Shìde, qǐngwèn nǐmen zhèlǐ yǒu shǒujī chōngdiànqì ma?
客人: 是的，请问你们这里有手机充电器吗？

前台 接待员: Qǐng tígōng yíxià nín xūyào chōngdiàn de shǒujī xínghào.
前台 接待员: 请提供一下您需要充电的手机型号。

客人: Huáwéi Mate 9.
客人: 华为 Mate 9。

前台 接待员: Hǎo de, máfan nín zài zhèbiān de zūjiè wùpǐndān shang dēngjì yíxià.
前台 接待员: 好的，麻烦您在这边的租借物品单上登记一下。

客人: Dēngjì hǎo le, yòngwán zhīhòu wǒ jiù guīhái huílai.
客人: 登记好了，用完之后我就归还回来。

前台 接待员: Méi wèntí, rúguǒ nín yǒu rènhé xūyào, qǐng suíshí liánxì wǒmen.
前台 接待员: 没问题，如果您有任何需要，请随时联系我们。

客人: Xièxie!
客人: 谢谢！

译文 yìwén Text in English

Guest: Hello! This is Li Ming in Room 801. My cell phone has run out of power.

Receptionist: Do you need the rental service?

Guest: Yes. Do you have a mobile phone charger?

Receptionist: Please tell me the phone model to be charged.

Guest: Huawei M9.

Receptionist: OK. Please register in the the rental list here.

Guest: All right, I'll return it when I've done with it.

Receptionist: No problem. If you need anything else, please feel free to contact us.

Guest: Thank you!

普通词语 pǔtōng cíyǔ General Vocabulary 🎧 08-02

1.	电	diàn	n.	(electric) power
2.	充电器	chōngdiànqì	n.	charger
	充电	chōng//diàn	v.	charge (a battery, etc.)

3.	型号	xínghào	n.	model, type
4.	归还	guīhuán	v.	return
5.	任何	rènhé	pron.	any
6.	随时	suíshí	adv.	anytime
7.	联系	liánxì	v.	contact

专业词语 zhuānyè cíyǔ Specialized Vocabulary 08-03

1.	租借	zūjiè	v.	rent
2.	租借物品单	zūjiè wùpǐndān	phr.	rental list
3.	华为	Huáwéi	pn.	Huawei, a leading global information and communications technology (ICT) solutions provider

B 08-04

客房中心: 这里是客房服务中心，有什么可以帮到您？

客人: 您好，我忘带转接头了，酒店提供租借服务吗？

客房中心: 提供的，请问您的姓名和房间号？

客人: 李华，我的房间号是508。

客房中心: 请稍等，我登记一下。需要为您送到房间吗？

客人: 好的，这是免费服务吗？

客房中心: 是的，住店客人免费租借。稍后客房服务员会把转接头给您送过去。

客人: 谢谢！

中文+酒店管理（中级）

译文 yìwén Text in English

Service Center: Room Service Center. What can I do for you?
Guest: Hello! I forgot to bring the adapter. Does the hotel provide rental service?
Service Center: Yes. Your name and room number, please.
Guest: Li Hua, and my room number is 508.
Service Center: Hold on, please. Let me register the information. Do you need it delivered to your room?
Guest: OK, is this service free?
Service Center: Yes, it's free of charge for hotel guests. The room attendant will bring it to you later.
Guest: Thank you!

普通词语 pǔtōng cíyǔ General Vocabulary 🎧 08-05

1.	中心	zhōngxīn	n.	center
2.	忘	wàng	v.	forget
3.	稍后	shāohòu	adv.	later on

专业词语 zhuānyè cíyǔ Specialized Vocabulary 🎧 08-06

转接头	zhuǎnjiētóu	n.	adapter

三、视听说 shì-tīng-shuō Viewing, Listening and Speaking

1. 观看总机员为客人办理租借服务的视频，将下列服务流程进行排序。
Watch the video about the telephone operator providing rental service for the guest and put the following service processes in order.

为 客人 提供 电熨斗 租借
wéi kèrén tígòng diànyùndǒu zūjiè
Renting an electric iron to the guest

① 登记客人信息
dēngjì kèrén xìnxī
Registering the information of the guest

② 安排租借服务
ānpái zūjiè fúwù
Arranging the rental service

③ 询问服务内容
xúnwèn fúwù nèiróng
Inquiring about the service included

④ 问候语
wènhòuyǔ
Greetings

96

租借物品服务 8
Rental Service

xúnwèn zūjiè wùpǐn
❺ 询问租借物品
Inquiring about the rented item

☐ → ☐ → ☐ → ☐ → ☐

2. 说一说   Let's talk.

练习说一说为客人提供租借服务的操作步骤及常用的服务用语。
Talk about the steps of providing rental service for the guest and the service expressions frequently used during the process.

四、学以致用　xuéyǐzhìyòng　Practicing What You Have Learnt

下雨天，客人向前台接待员询问酒店是否有雨伞，并询问如何租借。观看前台接待员为客人办理租借服务的视频，根据听到的内容选择正确选项。
On a rainy day, a guest goes to ask the receptionist if the hotel has an umbrella and how to rent it. Watch the video about the receptionist providing rental service for the guest, and choose the right answers based on what you hear.

yǔsǎn　zūjiè
雨伞 租借
Renting an Umbrella

kèrén:　Nǐ hǎo! Qǐngwèn jiǔdiàn yǒu　　　ma?
客人：你好！请问酒店有 ❶ 吗？

qiántái:　Nǐ hǎo!　yǒu de.
前台：你好！有的。

kèrén:　Wǒ kěyǐ jièyòng yì tiān ma?
客人：我可以借用一天吗？

qiántái:　Dāngrán kěyǐ.
前台：当然可以。

kèrén:　Xūyào　　　ma?
客人：需要 ❷ 吗？

qiántái:　Bù xūyào de,　zhǐ xūyào chūshì nín de shēnfèn　　　huò
前台：不需要的，只需要出示您的身份 ❸ 或 ❹ 。

kèrén:　Hǎo de,　xièxie.
客人：好的，谢谢。

97

qiántái: Bú kèqi!
前台：不客气！

A. yājīn 押金 deposit
B. yǔsǎn 雨伞 umbrella
C. fángkǎ 房卡 room card
D. zhèngjiàn 证件 credentials

五、小知识 xiǎo zhīshi Tips

酒店租借服务
Jiǔdiàn zūjiè fúwù

酒店除了标准的客房设备以外，还需购置一定数量的常用物品以满足客人的需求。这些物品的购置与配备一般随着酒店的档次高低而有所不同。酒店需要制定租借程序制度，物品的租借需要登记并每日跟踪记录，直到取回物品。一些酒店要求客人在租借物品单上签字，一些酒店要求客人付押金，如在离店时未将物品返还，押金不退还。一般，服务员不得直接接触现金。

Hotel Rental Service

In addition to normal room equipment, hotels also need to purchase a certain number of commonly used items to meet the needs of guests. The purchase and provision of these items generally vary depending on the hotel ratings. Hotels need to establish a rental procedure system. The rented items need to be registered and tracked daily until they are returned. Some hotels require guests to sign the list of rented items, while others require guests to pay a deposit. If the items are not returned when the guests check out, the deposit will not be refunded. In general, attendants are not allowed to have direct contact with cash.

租借物品服务
Rental Service

8

第二部分　Part 2

汉字　Chinese Characters

一、汉字知识　Hànzì zhīshi　Knowledge about Chinese Characters

1. 汉字的笔画（8）Strokes of Chinese characters (8)

笔画 Strokes	名称 Names	例字 Examples
ㄴ	竖弯 shùwān	四
ㄟ	横折弯 héngzhéwān	没

2. 汉字的结构（4）Structures of Chinese characters (4)

结构类型 Structure types	例字 Examples	结构图示 Illustrations
左右结构 Left-right structure	银 饭	⊟
左中右结构 Left-middle-right structure	班 微	⊞

二、汉字认读与书写　Hànzì rèndú yǔ shūxiě　The Recognition and Writing of Chinese Characters

认读下列词语，并试着读写构成词语的汉字。
Recognize the following words, and try to read and write the Chinese characters forming these words.

手机　　任何　　租借服务　　物品

手 机 任 何
租 借 服 务
物 　 品 　

第三部分　Part 3

日常用语　Daily Expressions

❶ 你不能这样。Nǐ bù néng zhèyàng. You can't be like that.
❷ 我马上就到。Wǒ mǎshàng jiù dào. I will be there right away.
❸ 让我想想。Ràng wǒ xiǎngxiang. Let me think.

99

第四部分　Part 4　单元实训　Unit Practical Training

模拟酒店租借物品服务
Simulated Rental Service in a Hotel

实训目的 Training purpose

通过本次实训，了解并掌握酒店租借物品服务的流程和服务用语。

Through the training, students will get to know and master proficiently the process of rental service in a hotel and the service expressions used during the process.

实训组织 Training organization

每组 2～3 人

2-3 students in each group

实训内容 Training content

某酒店客人需要租借物品，请安排租借服务。

Providing rental service for a hotel guest needing to rent something.

实训步骤 Training steps

❶ 教师将实训教室分成若干个虚拟的酒店前台和客房。

The teacher divides the classroom into several mimetic hotel receptions and guest rooms.

❷ 将参加实训的学员分成若干小组，每组 2～3 人。

Divide the students into groups of 2-3.

❸ 带领学员模拟酒店租借物品服务流程，过程中给予学员适当帮助。

Guide the students to make simulated process of rental service in a hotel and provide them with appropriate help during the process.

❹ 小组成员轮流扮演客人和前台接待员，练习并表演对话。

The group members take turns to play guests and receptionists, practicing and acting out the dialogs.

❺ 教师总结评价，实训结束。

The teacher makes a summary and evaluation, and ends the training.

第五部分　Part 5　单元小结　Unit Summary

词语 cíyǔ Vocabulary

普通词语　General Vocabulary

1.	电	diàn	n.	(electric) power
2.	充电器	chōngdiànqì	n.	charger
	充电	chōng//diàn	v.	charge (a battery, etc.)

词语 Vocabulary

3.	型号	xínghào	n.	model, type
4.	归还	guīhuán	v.	return
5.	任何	rènhé	pron.	any
6.	随时	suíshí	adv.	anytime
7.	联系	liánxì	v.	contact
8.	中心	zhōngxīn	n.	center
9.	忘	wàng	v.	forget
10.	稍后	shāohòu	adv.	later on

专业词语　Specialized Vocabulary

1.	租借	zūjiè	v.	rent
2.	租借物品单	zūjiè wùpǐndān	phr.	rental list
3.	华为	Huáwéi	pn.	Huawei, a leading global information and communications technology (ICT) solutions provider
4.	转接头	zhuǎnjiētóu	n.	adapter

句子 Sentences

1. 需要为您提供租借服务吗？
2. 请提供一下您需要充电的手机型号。
3. 麻烦您在这边的租借物品单上登记一下。
4. 如果您有任何需要，请随时联系我们。
5. 请问您的姓名和房间号。
6. 需要为您送到房间吗？
7. 住店客人免费租借。
8. 稍后客房服务员会把转接头给您送去。

9

Chéngshì jí lǚyóu xìnxī fúwù
城市及旅游信息服务
City and Tourism Information Service

chéngshì jí lǚyóu xìnxī fúwù
城市 及旅游信息服务
City and Tourism Information Service

jiāotōng fāngshì
交通 方式
Means of transportation

huòbì duìhuàn
货币兑换
Currency exchange

dìtú
地图
Maps

lǚyóu jìniànpǐn
旅游纪念品
Tourist souvenirs

lǚyóu jǐngdiǎn xìnxī
旅游景点 信息
Information about tourist attractions

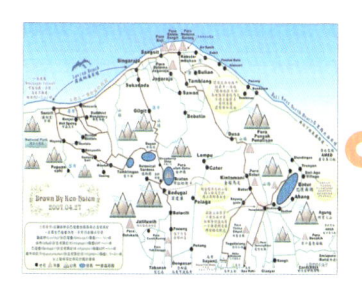

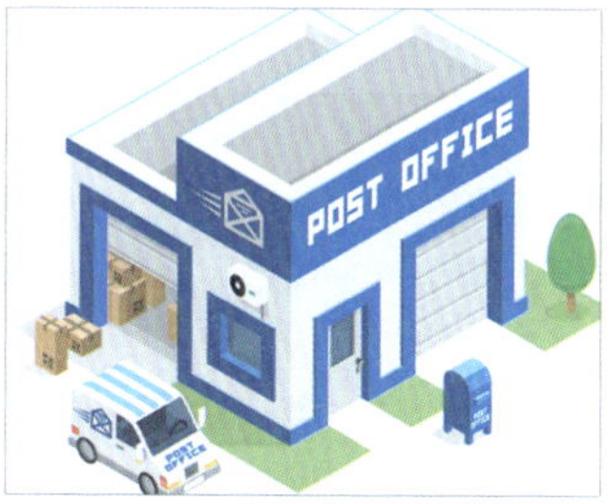

yóujú
邮局
Post offices

fàndiàn
饭店
Restaurants

103

题解　Introduction

1. 学习内容：酒店的城市及旅游信息服务相关流程和服务用语。
   Learning content: The process and service expressions related to the city and tourism information service of a hotel.

2. 知识目标：掌握城市及旅游信息服务相关的核心词语，学习汉字的笔画"ʓ""ㄣ"和全包围结构、半包围结构，学写本单元相关汉字。
   Knowledge objectives: To master the core vocabulary related to the city and tourism information service, learn the strokes "ʓ", "ㄣ", fully-enclosed structure and semi-enclosed structure of Chinese characters, and write the characters related to this unit.

3. 技能目标：能正确应对客人对城市及旅游信息服务方面的询问。
   Skill objective: To be able to properly respond to a guest's inquiries about the city and tourism information service.

第一部分　Part 1

课文　Texts

一、热身　rèshēn　Warm-up

1. 给词语选择对应的图片。　Choose the corresponding pictures for the words.

A

B

C

D

① huǒchē
火车 _____
train

② dìtiě
地铁 _____
subway

③ yóujú
邮局 _____
post office

④ jǐngqū
景区 _____
scenic spot

104

城市及旅游信息服务
City and Tourism Information Service

2. 观看视频，根据视频内容排列顺序。 Watch the video and put its content in order.

王 红 的 旅游 行程
Wáng Hóng de lǚyóu xíngchéng
Wang Hong's Itinerary

A. 公交车 gōngjiāochē — bus
B. 出租车 chūzūchē — taxi
C. 地图 dìtú — map
D. 门票 ménpiào — ticket
E. 机场 jīchǎng — airport
F. 博物馆 bówùguǎn — museum

☐ → ☐ → ☐ → ☐ → ☐ → ☐

二、课文 kèwén Texts

105

A 09-01

客人：请问，吴哥窟距离酒店多远？怎么去比较方便？

前台接待员：大约20公里，您可以乘坐出租车，半小时就到了。

客人：出租车费大概要多少元？

前台接待员：三万瑞尔，大约相当于50元人民币。

客人：好的，谢谢！柬埔寨还有哪些景区值得去，您能推荐一下吗？

前台接待员：金边王宫、塔山寺、万谷湖、巴肯山都很有名，您可以在酒店报一日游。

客人：我还想买一些东西，附近有超市吗？

前台接待员：您出酒店后左转，直行到第二个红绿灯路口再右转，在您右边就有一家大超市。

客人：好的，非常感谢。

译文 yìwén Text in English

Guest: How far is Angkor Wat from the hotel? What is the convenient way to get there?

Receptionist: It's about 20 kilometers away from here. You can take a taxi and get there in half an hour.

Guest: How much is the taxi fare?

Receptionist: Thirty thousand Riel. That's about 50 *yuan*.

Guest: OK, thanks! Can you recommend other scenic spots worth seeing in Cambodia?

Receptionist: The Royal Palace of Phnom Penh, Wat Phnom, Boeung Kak Lake and Phnom Bakheng are all very famous. You can sign up for a one-day tour at the hotel.

Guest: I'd like to buy some things. Is there a supermarket nearby?

城市及旅游信息服务
City and Tourism Information Service

Receptionist: When you get out of the hotel, turn left and go straight to the second crossing where there is a traffic light, and then turn right. There's a big supermarket on your right.
Guest: Great! Thank you very much.

普通词语 pǔtōng cíyǔ General Vocabulary 🎧 09-02

1.	吴哥窟	Wúgēkū	pn.	Angkor Wat
2.	多	duō	pron.	*used in questions to indicate degree/extent*
3.	远	yuǎn	adj.	far
4.	比较	bǐjiào	adv./v.	comparatively; compare
5.	大约	dàyuē	adv.	about
6.	公里	gōnglǐ	m.	kilometer
7.	乘坐	chéngzuò	v.	take (a taxi, train, boat, etc.)
8.	万	wàn	num.	ten thousand
9.	瑞尔	ruì'ěr	n.	Riel
10.	相当于	xiāngdāng yú	phr.	be equal to
	相当	xiāngdāng	v.	match, correspond to
11.	人民币	rénmínbì	n.	RMB
12.	哪些	nǎxiē	pron.	which, what
13.	值得	zhí//dé	v.	be worth
14.	金边王宫	Jīnbiān Wánggōng	pn.	the Royal Palace of Phnom Penh
15.	塔山寺	Tǎshān Sì	pn.	Wat Phnom
16.	万谷湖	Wàngǔ Hú	pn.	Boeung Kak Lake
17.	巴肯山	Bākěn Shān	pn.	Phnom Bakheng
18.	很	hěn	adv.	very
19.	有名	yǒu//míng	adj.	famous
20.	报名	bào//míng	v.	register, sign (up)
21.	买	mǎi	v.	buy
22.	一些	yìxiē	q.	some
23.	东西	dōngxi	n.	stuff, thing
24.	附近	fùjìn	n.	neighborhood
25.	超市	chāoshì	n.	supermarket
26.	左	zuǒ	n.	left
27.	转	zhuǎn	v.	turn
28.	红绿灯	hóng-lǜdēng	n.	traffic light
29.	路口	lùkǒu	n.	crossing

专业词语 zhuānyè cíyǔ Specialized Vocabulary 🎧 09-03

1.	距离	jùlí	n./v.	distance; be away from
2.	景区	jǐngqū	n.	scenic spot
3.	推荐	tuījiàn	v.	recommend
4.	一日游	yí rì yóu	phr.	one-day tour
5.	直行	zhí xíng	phr.	go straight

B 🎧 09-04

kèrén: Nín hǎo, wǒ xiǎng dào shìzhōngxīn, zěnme qù bǐjiào fāngbiàn?
客人：您好，我想到市中心，怎么去比较方便？

qiántái jiēdàiyuán: Nín kěyǐ zài jiǔdiàn ménkǒu chéngzuò dìtiě 1 hào xiàn zài Xīnjiēkǒu zhàn xià chē, huòzhě chéngzuò 3 lù gōngjiāochē zài Xīnjiēkǒu dōng zhàn xià chē.
前台 接待员：您可以在酒店门口乘坐地铁1号线在新街口站下车，或者乘坐3路公交车在新街口东站下车。

kèrén: Hǎo de, Xīnjiēkǒu yǒu shénme dà de shāngchǎng ma?
客人：好的，新街口有什么大的商场吗？

qiántái jiēdàiyuán: Nín kěyǐ qù guàng yí guàng Xīnjiēkǒu Bǎihuò Gōngsī, Zhōngyāng Shāngchǎng.
前台 接待员：您可以去逛一逛新街口百货公司、中央商场。

kèrén: Hǎo de, wǒ xiǎng mǎi yìxiē tèchǎn, nín yǒu shénme tuījiàn de ma?
客人：好的，我想买一些特产，您有什么推荐的吗？

qiántái jiēdàiyuán: Nín kěyǐ chángchang yǔhuāchá, yánshuǐyā, lìngwài nín yě kěyǐ xuǎngòu yìxiē Yúnjǐn xiǎo shìwù. Zhèxiē zài shìzhōngxīn de shāngchǎng dōu kěyǐ mǎidào.
前台 接待员：您可以尝尝雨花茶、盐水鸭，另外您也可以选购一些云锦小饰物。这些在市中心的商场都可以买到。

kèrén: Hǎo de, Xièxie!
客人：好的，谢谢！

译文 yìwén Text in English

Guest: Hello! I'd like to go to the downtown. How can I get there conveniently?
Receptionist: You can take Metro Line 1 or Bus No. 3 in front of the hotel and get off at Xinjiekou Stop.
Guest: OK. Is there a big shopping mall at Xinjiekou?
Receptionist: You can do some shopping at Xinjiekou Department Store and Central Emporium.
Guest: OK. I want to buy some specialities. What do you recommend?

9 城市及旅游信息服务
City and Tourism Information Service

Receptionist: You can try Yuhua Tea and salted ducks. In addition, you can also choose some brocade ornaments, which can be found in the downtown shopping malls.

Guest: OK, thank you!

普通词语 pǔtōng cíyǔ General Vocabulary 🎧 09-05

1.	市中心	shìzhōngxīn	n.	downtown
2.	门口	ménkǒu	n.	doorway
3.	新街口	Xīnjiēkǒu	pn.	Xinjiekou
4.	站	zhàn	n.	stop, station
5.	东	dōng	n.	east
6.	商场	shāngchǎng	n.	shopping mall
7.	逛	guàng	v.	stroll
8.	百货公司	bǎihuò gōngsī	phr.	department store
9.	中央	zhōngyāng	n.	center
10.	特产	tèchǎn	n.	speciality
11.	雨花茶	yǔhuāchá	pn.	Yuhua Tea
12.	盐水鸭	yánshuǐyā	pn.	salted duck
13.	另外	lìngwài	conj.	in addition
14.	云锦	Yúnjǐn	pn.	brocade
15.	小	xiǎo	adj.	small
16.	饰物	shìwù	n.	ornament
17.	这些	zhèxiē	pron.	these

专业词语 zhuānyè cíyǔ Specialized Vocabulary 🎧 09-06

1.	地铁	dìtiě	n.	metro, subway
2.	下车	xià chē	phr.	get off
3.	公交车	gōngjiāochē	n.	bus
4.	选购	xuǎngòu	v.	pick out and buy

三、视听说　shì-tīng-shuō　Viewing, Listening and Speaking

1. 观看客人询问前台接待员关于博物馆的视频，根据听到的内容选择正确选项。
Watch the video about the guest asking the receptionist about the museum, and choose the right answers based on what you hear.

❶ Kèrén xiǎng qù cānguān Guójiā＿＿＿＿＿，zuò chūzūchē dehuà dàgài＿＿＿＿＿fēnzhōng.
客人 想 去 参观 国家＿＿＿＿＿，坐 出租车 的话 大概＿＿＿＿＿分钟。
The guest wants to visit the National ＿＿＿＿. It will take ＿＿＿＿ minutes by taxi.

❷ Bówùguǎn＿＿＿＿＿tíngzhǐ shòupiào,＿＿＿＿＿diǎn guānmén.
博物馆＿＿＿＿＿停止 售票，＿＿＿＿＿点 关门。
The museum stops selling tickets at ＿＿＿＿ and closes at ＿＿＿＿.

❸ Bówùguǎn tígōng＿＿＿＿＿zhǒng yǔyán de jiǎngjiě fúwù.
博物馆 提供＿＿＿＿＿种 语言 的 讲解 服务。
The museum provides guide service in ＿＿＿＿ languages.

| A. sì 四 four | B. bówùguǎn 博物馆 museum | C. wǔ 五 five | D. 20 twenty | E. 4 diǎn bàn 4点半 four thirty |

2. 说一说　Let's talk.

练习说一说前台为客人提供博物馆参观信息时的对话。
Talk about how the receptionist provides about the museum for the guest.

城市及旅游信息服务 9
City and Tourism Information Service

四、学以致用　xuéyǐzhìyòng　Practicing What You Have Learnt

假如客人要从酒店出发去地铁站、邮局和医院，根据看到的内容选择正确的方位词。

Suppose a guest wants to start from the hotel to the subway station, post office and the hospital. Choose the correct location words based on what he/she sees.

dìtiězhàn
地铁站
Subway Station

A. zuǒ 左 left　　　B. yòu 右 right

① dìtiězhàn: 地铁站：Dìtiězhàn jiù zài wǒmen jiǔdiàn xié duìmiàn, nín chūmén _____ guǎi, zài lùkǒu guò gè mǎlù jiù dào le.
地铁站就在我们酒店斜对面，您出门_____拐，在路口过个马路就到了。

The subway station is diagonally opposite to our hotel. Go out of the hotel, turn _____ and cross the street.

② yóujú: 邮局：Cóng jiǔdiàn chūmén _____ guǎi, zài dì-yī gè lùkǒu jìxù _____ guǎi, zài zhí zǒu, yóujú zài nín de _____ shǒu biān.
从酒店出门_____拐，在第一个路口继续_____拐，再直走，邮局在您的_____手边。

Go out of the hotel and turn _____, turn _____ again at the first crossing, and then go straight along the street. The post office is on your _____.

③ yīyuàn: 医院：Cóng jiǔdiàn chūmén _____ guǎi, ránhòu zài dì-yī gè lùkǒu _____ guǎi, zài zhí zǒu, hěn kuài jiù néng kàndào, yīyuàn zài nín de zhèng qiánfāng.
从酒店出门_____拐，然后在第一个路口_____拐，再直走，很快就能看到，医院在您的正前方。

Turn _____ when you go out of the hotel, then turn _____ at the first crossing, go straight and you will see the hospital on your _____.

111

五、小知识　xiǎo zhīshi　Tips

旅游信息服务
Lǚyóu xìnxī fúwù

旅游信息服务是指宾馆、饭店、交通运输、餐饮娱乐、旅游购物及社会服务信息等，是旅游者特别关心的信息，也是决定游客此次旅行游览是否顺畅和满意的重要条件。考虑到各种不同层次的需求，酒店工作人员除了提供一般的旅游信息服务外，还要突出介绍涉外宾馆、特色餐饮、银行和应急等方面的信息。

Tourism Information Service

Tourism information service refers to providing information on hotels, restaurants, transportation, catering, entertainment, tourism, shopping and social service information, etc. It is the information tourists are particularly concerned about and determines whether their trips are smooth and satisfactory. Considering various needs of the tourists, hotel staff not only provides general tourism information service, but also highlights the information on hotels for foreigners, food specialties, banks and emergency disposal, etc.

第二部分　Part 2
汉字　Chinese Characters

一、汉字知识　Hànzì zhīshi　Knowledge about Chinese Characters

1. 汉字的笔画（9） Strokes of Chinese characters (9)

笔画 Strokes	名称 Names	例字 Examples
㇋	横折折撇 héngzhézhépiě	延、建
㇋	竖折撇 shùzhépiě	专

112

2. 汉字的结构（5） Structures of Chinese characters (5)

结构类型 Structure types	例字 Examples	结构图示 Illustrations
全包围结构 Fully-enclosed structure	国	□
半包围结构 Semi-enclosed structure	医 边 问 唐 凶	□ □ □ □ □

二、汉字认读与书写　Hànzì rèndú yǔ shūxiě　The Recognition and Writing of Chinese Characters

认读下列词语，并试着读写构成词语的汉字。

Recognize the following words, and try to read and write the Chinese characters forming these words.

怎么　　超市　　景区　　选购

| 怎 | | | | 么 | | | | 超 | | | | 市 | | | |
| 景 | | | | 区 | | | | 选 | | | | 购 | | | |

第三部分　Part 3

日常用语　Daily Expressions

❶ 我该怎么办？ Wǒ gāi zěnme bàn? What shall I do?

❷ 麻烦你告诉我他的电话号码。Máfan nǐ gàosu wǒ tā de diànhuà hàomǎ. Would you please tell me his phone number?

❸ 真不好意思，我忘了给你打电话。Zhēn bù hǎoyìsi, wǒ wàngle gěi nǐ dǎ diànhuà. Sorry, I forgot to phone you.

第四部分 Part 4 单元实训 Unit Practical Training

模拟城市及旅游信息服务
Simulated City and Tourism Information Service

实训目的 Training purpose
通过本次实训，了解并熟练掌握酒店的城市和旅游信息服务的基本服务流程和服务用语。
Through the training, students will get to know and proficiently master the basic service process and expressions used when the hotel provides city and tourism information.

实训组织 Training organization
每组 2～3 人
2-3 students in each group

实训内容 Training content
某酒店客人询问关于城市和旅游景点的详细信息，请安排相关服务。
Providing related service when a hotel guest asks for the detailed information on the city and the scenic spots.

实训步骤 Training steps
① 教师将实训教室分成若干个虚拟的酒店前台。
The teacher divides the classroom into several mimetic hotel receptions.
② 将参加实训的学员分成若干小组，每组 2～3 人。
Divide the students into groups of 2-3.
③ 带领学员模拟城市及旅游信息服务，过程中给予学员适当帮助。
Guide the students to simulate city and tourism information service, and provide them with appropriate assistance during the process.
④ 小组成员轮流扮演客人和前台接待员，练习并表演对话。
The group members take turns to play guests and receptionists, practicing and acting out the dialogs.
⑤ 教师总结评价，实训结束。
The teacher makes a summary and evaluation, and ends the training.

第五部分 Part 5 单元小结 Unit Summary

cíyǔ 词语 Vocabulary	普通词语 General Vocabulary				
	1.	吴哥窟	Wúgēkū	pn.	Angkor Wat
	2.	多	duō	pron.	used in questions to indicate degree/extent
	3.	远	yuǎn	adj.	far

词语 cíyǔ Vocabulary

4.	比较	bǐjiào	adv./v.	comparatively; compare
5.	大约	dàyuē	adv.	about
6.	公里	gōnglǐ	m.	kilometer
7.	乘坐	chéngzuò	v.	take (a taxi, train, boat, etc.)
8.	万	wàn	num.	ten thousand
9.	瑞尔	ruì'ěr	n.	Riel
10.	相当于	xiāngdāng yú	phr.	be equal to
	相当	xiāngdāng	v.	match, correspond to
11.	人民币	rénmínbì	n.	RMB
12.	哪些	nǎxiē	pron.	which, what
13.	值得	zhí//dé	v.	be worth
14.	金边王宫	Jīnbiān Wánggōng	pn.	the Royal Palace of Phnom Penh
15.	塔山寺	Tǎshān Sì	pn.	Wat Phnom
16.	万谷湖	Wàngǔ Hú	pn.	Boeung Kak Lake
17.	巴肯山	Bākěn Shān	pn.	Phnom Bakheng
18.	很	hěn	adv.	very
19.	有名	yǒu//míng	adj.	famous
20.	报名	bào//míng	v.	register, sign (up)
21.	买	mǎi	v.	buy
22.	一些	yìxiē	q.	some
23.	东西	dōngxi	n.	stuff, thing
24.	附近	fùjìn	n.	neighborhood
25.	超市	chāoshì	n.	supermarket
26.	左	zuǒ	n.	left
27.	转	zhuǎn	v.	turn
28.	红绿灯	hóng-lǜdēng	n.	traffic light
29.	路口	lùkǒu	n.	crossing
30.	市中心	shìzhōngxīn	n.	downtown
31.	门口	ménkǒu	n.	doorway
32.	新街口	Xīnjiēkǒu	pn.	Xinjiekou
33.	站	zhàn	n.	stop, station

cíyǔ 词语 Vocabulary

34.	东	dōng	n.	east
35.	商场	shāngchǎng	n.	shopping mall
36.	逛	guàng	v.	stroll
37.	百货公司	bǎihuò gōngsī	phr.	department store
38.	中央	zhōngyāng	n.	center
39.	特产	tèchǎn	n.	speciality
40.	雨花茶	yǔhuāchá	pn.	Yuhua Tea
41.	盐水鸭	yánshuǐyā	pn.	salted duck
42.	另外	lìngwài	conj.	in addition
43.	云锦	Yúnjǐn	pn.	brocade
44.	小	xiǎo	adj.	small
45.	饰物	shìwù	n.	ornament
46.	这些	zhèxiē	pron.	these

专业词语 Specialized Vocabulary

1.	距离	jùlí	n./v.	distance; be away from
2.	景区	jǐngqū	n.	scenic spot
3.	推荐	tuījiàn	v.	recommend
4.	一日游	yí rì yóu	phr.	one-day tour
5.	直行	zhí xíng	phr.	go straight
6.	地铁	dìtiě	n.	metro, subway
7.	下车	xià chē	phr.	get off
8.	公交车	gōngjiāochē	n.	bus
9.	选购	xuǎngòu	v.	pick out and buy

jùzi 句子 Sentences

1. 大约20公里，您可以乘坐出租车，半小时就到了。
2. 三万瑞尔，大约相当于50元人民币。
3. 您可以在酒店报一日游。
4. 您出酒店后左转，直行到第二个红绿灯路口再右转。
5. 在您右边就有一家大超市。
6. 您可以在酒店门口乘坐地铁1号线在新街口站下车，或者乘坐3路公交车在新街口东站下车。
7. 您可以去逛一逛新街口百货公司、中央商场。
8. 您可以尝尝雨花茶、盐水鸭。
9. 您也可以选购一些云锦小饰物，这些在市中心的商场都可以买到。

10 Tuánduì tuì fáng fúwù
团队退房服务
Group Check-out Service

tuánduì tuì fáng fúwù liúchéng
团队退房服务流程
Group Check-out Service Process

cháxún rùzhù qījiān qítā xiāofèi xiàngmù
查询入住期间其他消费项目
Checking other consumption items during the guests' stay

tōngzhī cháfáng
通知查房
Having the room checked

bànlǐ tuì fáng shǒuxù (zhuǎnjiāo yíliú wùpǐn,
办理退房手续（转交遗留物品、
péicháng sǔnhuài wùpǐn děng)
赔偿损坏物品等）
Going through check-out procedure (handing over the items left and compensating for the damaged items, etc.)

zhìxiè, sòngkè
致谢、送客
Expressing gratitude and seeing off guests

117

题解　Introduction

1. 学习内容：酒店团队客人退房的流程和服务用语。
   Learning content: The process and service expressions for group guests to check out of a hotel.
2. 知识目标：掌握团队客人退房相关的核心词语，学习汉字的笔画（总表）、笔顺（总表）和结构（总表），学写本单元相关汉字。
   Knowledge objectives: To master the core vocabulary related to group guest check-out, learn the general tables of strokes, stroke orders and structures of Chinese characters, and write the characters related to this unit.
3. 技能目标：能为团队客人办理退房服务。
   Skill objective: To be able to provide check-out service for group guests.

第一部分　Part 1

课文　Texts

一、热身　rèshēn　Warm-up

1. 给词语选择对应的图片。　Choose the corresponding pictures for the words.

A

B

C

D

① lǐngduì
领队 _____
tour leader

② lǚyóu tuánduì
旅游 团队 _____
tour group

③ huìyì
会议 _____
conference

④ lǚxíngshè
旅行社 _____
travel agency

118

团队退房服务 **10**
Group Check-out Service

2. 观看视频，根据视频内容选择正确选项。
Watch the video and choose the right answer based on the video.

wèntí: Gāi shìpín zhōng miáoshù de zhīfù fāngshì shì
问题：该视频 中 描述 的 支付 方式 是 _____。
Question: The mode of payment showed in this video is _____.

        xiànjīn zhīfù   guàzhàng
  A. 现金支付   B. 挂账
    cash payment   city ledger

二、课文 kèwén Texts

A 🎧 10-01

lǚxíngtuán lǐngduì: Nín hǎo, wǒ shì Chén Lì, Zhōngguó Guójì Lǚxíngshè de lǐngduì. Wǒ xiǎng
旅行团 领队：您好，我是陈丽，中国 国际旅行社的领队。我 想

gěi wǒmen de tuánduì tuì fáng.
给 我们的团队 退房。

qiántái jiēdàiyuán: Hǎo de, qǐng gàosu wǒ nín de fángjiānhào.
前台 接待员：好的，请告诉我您的房间号。

lǚxíngtuán lǐngduì: 1515 dào 1518, gòng sì jiān fáng, cóng 5 yuè 8 hào qǐ rùzhù de.
旅行团 领队：1515 到 1518，共四间 房，从 5月 8号起入住的。

119

Zhèxiē shì fángkǎ.
这些是房卡。

qiántái jiēdàiyuán: Hǎo de, qǐng shāo děng. Wǒ lái dǎyìn zhàngdān míngxì gěi nín. Nín yígòng
前台 接待员： 好的，请稍等。我来打印账单明细给您。您一共
xūyào fù 880 měiyuán, qǐng nín héduì. Duì le, 1516 fángjiān de
需要付880美元，请您核对。对了，1516房间的
diànhuàfèi hái méiyǒu jiéqīng.
电话费还没有结清。

lǚxíngtuán lǐngduì: Diànhuàfèi kèrén zìjǐ fù. Tā kěnéng wàng le, wǒ lái gàosu tā.
旅行团 领队： 电话费客人自己付。他可能忘了，我来告诉他。

qiántái jiēdàiyuán: Xièxie, Chén nǚshì. Qǐng nín zài zhàngdān shang qiānzì. Qǐngwèn zěnme
前台 接待员： 谢谢，陈女士。请您在账单上签字。请问怎么
zhīfù?
支付？

lǚxíngtuán lǐngduì: Xìnyòngkǎ zhīfù.
旅行团 领队： 信用卡支付。

qiántái jiēdàiyuán: Xièxie, zhè shì nín de fāpiào. Qīdài nín de zàicì guānglín.
前台 接待员： 谢谢，这是您的发票。期待您的再次光临。

译文 yìwén Text in English

Tour leader: Hello! I'm Chen Li, the tour leader of China International Travel Service. I'd like to check out for my group.

Receptionist: OK. Your room numbers, please.

Tour leader: There were four rooms from 1515 to 1518 checked in starting May 8th. Here are the room cards.

Receptionist: OK, just a moment, please. Let me print the bill details for you. Your total charge is $880. Please have a check. By the way, the phone bill of Room 1516 is still unpaid.

Tour leader: The guest will take care of the bill himself. He probably forgot it. I'll tell him.

Receptionist: Thank you, Ms. Chen. Please sign the bill. How would you like to pay?

Tour leader: By credit card.

Receptionist: Thank you. Here is your invoice. We're looking forward to serving you again.

普通词语 pǔtōng cíyǔ General Vocabulary   10-02

1.	从……起	cóng…qǐ	phr.	from
2.	打印	dǎyìn	v.	print
3.	一共	yígòng	adv.	altogether
4.	美元	měiyuán	n.	US dollar

| 5. | 核对 | héduì | v. | check |
| 6. | 电话费 | diànhuàfèi | phr. | phone bill |

专业词语 zhuānyè cíyǔ Specialized Vocabulary 🎧 10-03

1.	明细	míngxì	adj.	clear and detailed
2.	结清	jiéqīng	phr.	settle, square up
3.	发票	fāpiào	n.	invoice

B 🎧 10-04

客人：你好，我是参加"中—柬 友好合作会议"的负责人张山，我来给参会的客人办理退房。

前台接待员：张先生，你们一共五间会议用房，都是您来结账，对吗？

客人：是的，房卡给您。

前台接待员：贵公司是我们挂账协议用户，您有权限挂单结账，请给我您的护照。

客人：802房间的酒水费和805房间的洗衣费由客人自己支付，我会通知他们。

前台接待员：这是您的账单。没有问题的话，请签字。

客人：好的，给您。

前台接待员：好的，这是您的挂账单和账单明细，请收好。

客人：谢谢。

译文 yìwén Text in English

Guest: Hello! I'm Zhang Shan, the person in charge of the China-Cambodia Friendship and Cooperation Conference. I'm here to check out the guests.

Receptionist: Mr. Zhang, you have five conference rooms. You'll pay the bill of all, right?

Guest: Yes, and here are the room cards.

Receptionist: Your company is our city ledger agreement user and you have the right to pay via city ledger. Your passport, please.

Guest: The drinks of Room 802 and laundry charge of Room 805 are to be paid by the guests themselves. I will inform them.

Receptionist: Here is your bill. If there are no problems, please sign your name.

Guest: OK, here you are.

Receptionist: OK. Here is your city ledger bill and billing details. Please keep them well.

Guest: Thank you.

普通词语 pǔtōng cíyǔ General Vocabulary 10-05

1.	参加	cānjiā	v.	participate
2.	会议	huìyì	n.	conference
3.	负责人	fùzérén	n.	person in charge
	负责	fùzé	v./adj.	be responsible for; responsible
4.	用户	yònghù	n.	user
5.	通知	tōngzhī	v./n.	inform, notify; notice
6.	……的话	…dehuà	part.	used at the end of a conditional clause

专业词语 zhuānyè cíyǔ Specialized Vocabulary 10-06

1.	会议用房	huìyì yòng fáng	phr.	conference room
2.	协议	xiéyì	n.	agreement
3.	权限	quánxiàn	n.	right, permission
4.	挂单	guàdān	v.	pend the order
5.	酒水费	jiǔshuǐfèi	phr.	beverage charge
6.	洗衣费	xǐyīfèi	phr.	laundry charge
7.	挂账单	guàzhàngdān	n.	city ledger bill

三、视听说 shì-tīng-shuō Viewing, Listening and Speaking

1. 观看前台接待员为领队办理团队客人退房的视频，将下列服务流程进行排序。
Watch the video about the receptionist helping the tour leader check the group of guests, and arrange the following service processes in order.

① Máfan nín tōngzhī kèrén jiéqīng.
麻烦您通知客人结清。
Please inform the guest to settle it.

② Nǐmen shì 6 yuè 3 hào rùzhù de.
你们是6月3号入住的。
You checked in on June 3rd.

③ Zhè shì nín de zhàngdān, qǐng quèrèn.
这是您的账单，请确认。
This is the bill for your confirmation.

④ 608 fángjiān yǒu yì bǐ diànhuàfèi 80 yuán.
608房间有一笔电话费80元。
There is a phone bill of 80 *yuan* for Room 608.

⑤ Fángkǎ dōu shōuqí le ma?
房卡都收齐了吗？
Have you collected all the room cards?

⑥ Měi jiān fáng jiàgé shì 500 yuán/ wǎn.
每间房价格是500元/晚。
The rate for each room is 500 *yuan* per night.

☐ ⇒ ☐ ⇒ ☐ ⇒ ☐ ⇒ ☐ ⇒ ☐

2. 说一说 Let's talk.

练习说一说为团队客人办理退房时的服务用语。　Practice the service expressions for group check-out.

四、学以致用 xuéyǐzhìyòng　Practicing What You Have Learnt

观看视频，根据视频内容完成下列酒店客房账单明细。
Watch the video and complete the following hotel billing details based on the video.

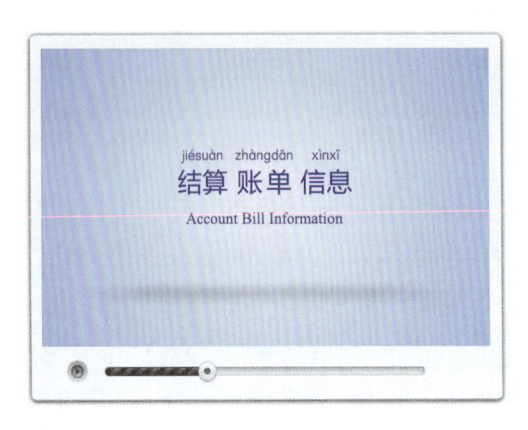

jiésuàn zhàngdān xìnxī
结算 账单 信息
Account Bill Information

jiǔdiàn kèfáng zhàngdān míngxì
酒店 客房 账单 明细
Hotel Room Bills

gōngsī 公司 Company		guójí 国籍 Nationality	Zhōngguó 中国 Chinese	
tuánduì lèixíng 团队 类型 Type of the group	tuánduì 团队 Group		huìyì 会议 √ Conference	
dǐ diàn rìqī 抵店日期 Check-in date				
lí diàn rìqī 离店日期 Check-out date				
fángjiān lèixíng 房间 类型 Room types	biāozhǔnjiān 标准间 Standard	dàchuángfáng 大床房 Queen room	háohuá tàojiān 豪华 套间 Deluxe suite	héjì yuán 合计（元） Total（RMB）
fángjiān shùliàng 房间 数量 Number of rooms		2		
fángjiān dānjià yuán/wǎn 房间 单价（元/晚） Room rate	380			

124

（续表）

酒店客房账单明细 Hotel Room Bills				
支付方式 Payment	现金 Cash	信用卡 Credit card	支票 Check	挂账 City ledger
客人签字 Signature of the guest				

五、小知识 xiǎo zhīshi Tips

团队客人退房手续 Tuánduì kèrén tuì fáng shǒuxù

如果是团队客人统一退房，酒店前台工作人员应注意提前做好准备，通知客房服务中心，提高退房效率。如果是分散退房，要对客人退回来的房卡进行房号核对，并确认是还一卡还是退整个房间。房间有偿消费部分或需要客人赔偿的费用一般由客人自行承担，按酒店的正常手续进行收取。

Group Check-out Formalities

In the case of a group check-out, the hotel receptionist should prepare in advance and inform the room service center to improve check-out efficiency. In the case of decentralized check-out, check the returned room cards against the room numbers, and make sure whether a single card is returned or the whole room is checked out. The paid items or compensation costs are generally paid by the guests themselves according to the normal formalities of the hotel.

第二部分　Part 2　汉字　Chinese Characters

一、汉字知识　Hànzì zhīshi　Knowledge about Chinese Characters

1. 汉字的笔画（总表）Strokes of Chinese characters (general table)

一	丨	丿	丶	丶	㇆	㇗
㇉	一	亅	丿	乚	乀	丨
㇈	㇂	㇏	㇀	㇅	乙	㇋
㇌	㇊	㇁	乀	㇃	㇉	㇄

2. 汉字的笔顺（总表）Stroke orders of Chinese characters (general table)

笔顺规则 Rules of stroke orders	例字 Examples
先横后竖	十
先撇后捺	人、八
先上后下	三
先左后右	人
先中间后两边	小
先外边后里边	问
先外后里再封口	国、日

3. 汉字的结构（总表）Structures of Chinese characters (general table)

类型 Structure types	结构图示 Illustrations	例字 Examples
独体结构	□	生、不
品字形结构	⊟	品
上下结构	☐ ☐	爸、学
上中下结构	☰	意
左右结构	☐	银、饭
左中右结构	‖‖	班、微
全包围结构	☐	国
半包围结构	☐ ☐ ☐ ☐ ☐	医、边、问、唐、凶

126

二、汉字认读与书写　Hànzì rèndú yǔ shūxiě　The Recognition and Writing of Chinese Characters

认读下列词语，并试着读写构成词语的汉字。
Recognize the following words, and try to read and write the Chinese characters forming these words.

账单明细　　团队退房　　挂账　　发票

账				单			明			细		
团				队			退			房		
挂				账			发			票		

第三部分　Part 3
日常用语　Daily Expressions

❶ 谢谢你的礼物，我很喜欢。Xièxie nǐ de lǐwù, wǒ hěn xǐhuan. Thanks for your gift. I like it very much.

❷ 谢谢您的邀请，我一定去。Xièxie nín de yāoqǐng, wǒ yídìng qù. Thanks for your invitation. I will go for sure.

❸ 我该走了，再见。Wǒ gāi zǒu le, zàijiàn. I've got to go. Bye.

第四部分　Part 4
单元实训　Unit Practical Training

模拟酒店团队退房服务
Simulated Group Check-out Service in a Hotel

实训目的 Training purpose

通过本次实训，了解并熟练掌握酒店的团队退房服务基本流程和服务用语。
Through the training, students will get to know and master proficiently the basic process of group check-out in a hotel and the service expressions used during the process.

实训组织 Training organization

每组 2～3 人
2-3 students in each group

实训内容 Training content

某公司在酒店举行了会议，请根据客房的实际情况，办理退房服务，并询问房间信息及结账方式等。

A company held a meeting in a hotel. Please provide check-out service, asking for the information about the rooms and the method of payment based on the situations of the guest rooms.

实训步骤 Training steps

❶ 教师将实训教室分成若干个虚拟的酒店前台。

The teacher divides the classroom into several mimetic hotel receptions.

❷ 将参加实训的学员分成若干组，每组 2～3 人。

Divide the students into groups of 2-3.

❸ 带领学员模拟酒店团队退房服务，过程中给予学员适当帮助。

Guide students to simulate the group check-out service in a hotel, and provide them with appropriate assistance during the process.

❹ 小组成员轮流扮演客人和前台接待员，练习并表演对话。

The group members take turns to play guests and receptionists, practicing and acting out the dialogs.

❺ 教师总结评价，实训结束。

The teacher makes a summary and evaluation, and ends the training.

第五部分　Part 5　单元小结　Unit Summary

词语 cíyǔ Vocabulary

普通词语　General Vocabulary

1.	从……起	cóng…qǐ	phr.	from
2.	打印	dǎyìn	v.	print
3.	一共	yígòng	adv.	altogether
4.	美元	měiyuán	n.	US dollar
5.	核对	héduì	v.	check
6.	电话费	diànhuàfèi	phr.	phone bill
7.	参加	cānjiā	v.	participate
8.	会议	huìyì	n.	conference
9.	负责人	fùzérén	n.	person in charge
	负责	fùzé	v./adj.	be responsible for; responsible
10.	用户	yònghù	n.	user
11.	通知	tōngzhī	v./n.	inform, notify; notice
12.	……的话	…dehuà	part.	*used at the end of a conditional clause*

团队退房服务
Group Check-out Service

10

专业词语　Specialized Vocabulary

cíyǔ 词语 Vocabulary

1.	明细	míngxì	adj.	clear and detailed
2.	结清	jiéqīng	phr.	settle, square up
3.	发票	fāpiào	n.	invoice
4.	会议用房	huìyì yòng fáng	phr.	conference room
5.	协议	xiéyì	n.	agreement
6.	权限	quánxiàn	n.	right, permission
7.	挂单	guàdān	v.	pend the order
8.	酒水费	jiǔshuǐfèi	phr.	beverage charge
9.	洗衣费	xǐyīfèi	phr.	laundry charge
10.	挂账单	guàzhàngdān	n.	city ledger bill

jùzi 句子 Sentences

1. 我来打印账单明细给您。
2. 您一共需要付880美元，请您核对。
3. 对了，1516房间的电话费还没有结清。
4. 请您在账单上签字。请问您怎么支付？
5. 这是您的发票。期待您的再次光临。
6. 你们一共五间会议用房，都是您来结账，对吗？

附录　Appendixes

词汇总表　Vocabulary

序号	生词	拼音	词性	词义	普通G/专业S	所属单元
1	按钮	ànniǔ	n.	button	S	6A
2	按时	ànshí	adv.	on time	G	7A
3	巴肯山	Bākěn Shān	pn.	Phnom Bakheng	G	9A
4	巴士	bāshì	n.	bus	G	2A
5	百货公司	bǎihuò gōngsī	phr.	department store	G	9B
6	帮忙	bāng//máng	v.	help	G	6A
7	棒	bàng	adj.	great, wonderful	G	6A
8	报名	bào//míng	v.	register, sign (up)	G	9A
9	本来	běnlái	adj./adv.	original; originally	G	4B
10	比较	bǐjiào	adv./v.	comparatively; compare	G	9A
11	笔记本电脑	bǐjìběn diànnǎo	phr.	laptop	S	6A
12	变化	biànhuà	v./n.	change	G	2A
13	不好意思	bù hǎoyìsi	phr.	sorry	G	4B
14	参加	cānjiā	v.	participate	G	10B
15	层	céng	m.	floor	G	2A
16	茶	chá	n.	tea	G	7A
17	尝	cháng	v.	try, taste	G	1A
18	超市	chāoshì	n.	supermarket	G	9A
19	吵	chǎo	adj.	noisy	G	3B
20	称呼	chēnghu	v./n.	call; appellation	G	2A
21	成员	chéngyuán	n.	member	G	2A
22	城景房	chéngjǐngfáng	n.	city view room	S	3B
23	乘坐	chéngzuò	v.	take (a taxi, train, boat, etc.)	G	9A
24	充电	chōng//diàn	v.	charge (a battery, etc.)	G	8A
25	充电器	chōngdiànqì	n.	charger	G	8A
26	从……起	cóng…qǐ	phr.	from	G	10A
27	打算	dǎsuàn	v.	plan, intend	G	4B
28	打印	dǎyìn	v.	print	G	10A
29	大约	dàyuē	adv.	about	G	9A
30	带	dài	v.	be with, have (sth.) attached	G	2A

（续表）

序号	生词	拼音	词性	词义	普通G/专业S	所属单元
31	倒	dào	v.	pour	G	7B
32	……的话	…dehuà	part.	used at the end of a conditional clause	G	10B
33	登记表	dēngjìbiǎo	n.	registration form	S	2A
34	等候	děnghòu	v.	wait	G	3A
35	地方	dìfang	n.	place	G	6B
36	地铁	dìtiě	n.	metro, subway	S	9B
37	第	dì	pref.	a prefix indicating ordinal numbers	G	2A
38	点	diǎn	v.	order, ask for sth. to eat or drink in a restaurant, bar, etc.	G	7A
39	点击	diǎnjī	v.	click	S	6A
40	电	diàn	n.	(electric) power	G	8A
41	电话费	diànhuàfèi	phr.	phone bill	G	10A
42	电脑	diànnǎo	n.	computer	S	6A
43	调换	diàohuàn	v.	exchange, swap	S	3A
44	东	dōng	n.	east	G	9B
45	东西	dōngxi	n.	stuff, thing	G	9A
46	对	duì	m.	a measure word for people, animals, etc.	G	2A
47	对	duì	v.	towards	G	3B
48	多	duō	pron.	used in questions to indicate degree/extent	G	9A
49	发票	fāpiào	n.	invoice	S	10A
50	反	fǎn	adj.	opposite	G	3B
51	方向	fāngxiàng	n.	direction	G	3B
52	访问	fǎngwèn	v.	visit	G	3A
53	放	fàng	v.	put	G	7B
54	费用	fèiyong	n.	cost, fee	G	2B
55	分给	fēn gěi	phr.	distribute	G	2B
56	份	fèn	m.	share, portion	G	7A
57	夫妇	fūfù	n.	husband and wife, couple	G	2A
58	付	fù	v.	pay	G	4A
59	付款	fùkuǎn	v.	pay a sum of money	S	2B
60	负责	fùzé	v./adj.	be responsible for; responsible	G	10B
61	负责人	fùzérén	n.	person in charge	G	10B
62	附近	fùjìn	n.	neighborhood	G	9A

131

(续表)

序号	生词	拼音	词性	词义	普通G/专业S	所属单元
63	改	gǎi	v.	change	G	6B
64	感谢	gǎnxiè	v.	thank	G	4B
65	更改	gēnggǎi	v.	change	G	6B
66	公共	gōnggòng	adj.	public	G	6B
67	公交车	gōngjiāochē	n.	bus	S	9B
68	公里	gōnglǐ	m.	kilometer	G	9A
69	供	gōng	v.	provide sth. for (the use or convenience of)	G	7A
70	共	gòng	adv.	altogether	G	2A
71	挂单	guàdān	v.	pend the order	S	10B
72	挂账	guà//zhàng	v.	pay by city ledger	S	7B
73	挂账单	guàzhàngdān	n.	city ledger bill	S	10B
74	逛	guàng	v.	stroll	G	9B
75	归还	guīhuán	v.	return	G	8A
76	贵重	guìzhòng	adj.	valuable	G	5B
77	国际	guójì	n.	internationality	G	2A
78	过	guò	v.	spend (time), pass (time)	G	5A
79	喝	hē	v.	drink	G	7A
80	核对	héduì	v.	check	G	10A
81	核实	héshí	v.	verify	G	4A
82	很	hěn	adv.	very	G	9A
83	红酒	hóngjiǔ	n.	red wine	G	7A
84	红绿灯	hónglǜdēng	n.	traffic light	G	9A
85	壶	hú	m.	pot	G	7A
86	花园	huāyuán	n.	garden	G	3B
87	华为	Huáwéi	pn.	Huawei, a leading global information and communications technology (ICT) solutions provider	S	8A
88	换	huàn	v.	exchange	S	3A
89	会客厅	huìkètīng	n.	living room	S	3A
90	会议	huìyì	n.	conference	G	10B
91	会议室	huìyìshì	n.	conference room	S	1B
92	会议用房	huìyì yòng fáng	phr.	conference room	S	10B
93	鸡肉饭	jīròufàn	phr.	chicken rice	G	7A

（续表）

序号	生词	拼音	词性	词义	普通 G/专业 S	所属单元
94	柬埔寨	Jiǎnpǔzhài	pn.	Cambodia	S	2A
95	件	jiàn	m.	*a measure word for countable nouns*	G	5B
96	健身房	jiànshēnfáng	n.	gym	S	1B
97	将	jiāng	adv./prep.	*used to indicate an imminent/a future occurrence*; with, by	G	2A
98	接入	jiērù	phr.	have access to	G	6A
99	结清	jiéqīng	phr.	settle, square up	S	10A
100	结账	jié//zhàng	v.	check out	G	7B
101	介意	jiè//yì	v.	mind	G	4B
102	金边王宫	Jīnbiān Wánggōng	pn.	the Royal Palace of Phnom Penh	G	9A
103	进	jìn	v.	enter	G	7B
104	景区	jǐngqū	n.	scenic spot	S	9A
105	酒水费	jiǔshuǐfèi	phr.	beverage charge	S	10B
106	距离	jùlí	n./v.	distance; be away from	S	9A
107	咖啡	kāfēi	n.	coffee	G	7A
108	可用	kě yòng	phr.	available	G	6A
109	客房	kèfáng	n.	guest room	S	3A
110	客户	kèhù	n.	client	G	3A
111	来	lái	v.	come	G	5B
112	离店	lí diàn	phr.	check out	S	2B
113	里面	lǐmiàn	n.	inside	G	6B
114	理解	lǐjiě	v.	understand	G	4B
115	连接	liánjiē	v.	connect	G	6A
116	联系	liánxì	v.	contact	G	8A
117	列表	lièbiǎo	n.	list	G	6A
118	领队	lǐngduì	n.	(tour) leader	S	2A
119	领取	lǐngqǔ	v.	collect, pick up	G	4B
120	另外	lìngwài	conj.	in addition	G	9B
121	楼	lóu	n.	floor	G	1A
122	路口	lùkǒu	n.	crossing	G	9A
123	旅行社	lǚxíngshè	n.	travel agency	S	2A
124	旅行团	lǚxíngtuán	n.	travel group	S	2A
125	绿茶	lǜchá	n.	green tea	G	7A

133

（续表）

序号	生词	拼音	词性	词义	普通G/专业S	所属单元
126	麻烦	máfan	v./adj.	trouble; troublesome	G	2B
127	马路	mǎlù	n.	road	G	3B
128	买	mǎi	v.	buy	G	9A
129	美元	měiyuán	n.	US dollar	G	10A
130	门口	ménkǒu	n.	doorway	G	9B
131	密码	mìmǎ	n.	password	G	6A
132	免费	miǎn//fèi	v.	be free (of charge)	G	6B
133	面对	miànduì	v.	face	G	3B
134	名称	míngchēng	n.	name	G	6A
135	名字	míngzi	n.	name	G	2A
136	明细	míngxì	adj.	clear and detailed	S	10A
137	哪些	nǎxiē	pron.	which, what	G	9A
138	男士	nánshì	n.	man	G	2A
139	牛肉面	niúròumiàn	phr.	beef noodles	G	7A
140	其他	qítā	pron.	other	G	5A
141	签	qiān	v.	sign, write one's signature	G	2B
142	签证	qiānzhèng	n.	visa	S	2B
143	请进	qǐng jìn	phr.	Please come in.	G	7B
144	权限	quánxiàn	n.	right, permission	S	10B
145	人民币	rénmínbì	n.	RMB	G	9A
146	任何	rènhé	pron.	any	G	8A
147	任务栏	rènwulán	n.	taskbar	S	6A
148	瑞尔	ruì'ěr	n.	Riel	G	9A
149	商场	shāngchǎng	n.	shopping mall	G	9B
150	上	shang	n.	used after a noun to indicate the surface of sth.	G	2A
151	上网	shàng//wǎng	v.	surf the Internet	G	6A
152	稍后	shāohòu	adv.	later on	G	8B
153	设置	shèzhì	v.	set, set up	S	6B
154	申请	shēnqǐng	v.	apply	S	4B
155	食物	shíwù	n.	food	G	1A
156	使用	shǐyòng	v.	use	G	6B
157	市中心	shìzhōngxīn	n.	downtown	G	9B

（续表）

序号	生词	拼音	词性	词义	普通G/专业S	所属单元
158	饰物	shìwù	n.	ornament	G	9B
159	试	shì	v.	try	G	6B
160	收好	shōuhǎo	phr.	keep well	G	2B
161	收据	shōujù	n.	receipt	S	4A
162	手机	shǒujī	n.	mobile phone	G	6B
163	送餐	sòng cān	phr.	deliver meals	S	7A
164	送餐员	sòngcānyuán	n.	delivery man	S	7A
165	随后	suíhòu	adv.	then	G	5A
166	随时	suíshí	adv.	anytime	G	8A
167	所有	suǒyǒu	adj.	all	G	6B
168	塔山寺	Tǎshān Sì	pn.	Wat Phnom	G	9A
169	太	tài	adv.	too, excessively	G	6A
170	套餐	tàocān	n.	combo, set meal	S	7A
171	特产	tèchǎn	n.	speciality	G	9B
172	填写	tiánxiě	v.	fill in	G	2A
173	通常	tōngcháng	adj.	usually	G	6A
174	通知	tōngzhī	v./n.	inform, notify; notice	G	10B
175	同一层	tóng yì céng	phr.	the same floor	S	2B
176	统一	tǒngyī	adj.	unified	G	2B
177	图标	túbiāo	n.	icon	S	6A
178	团队	tuánduì	n.	team, group	G	2A
179	推荐	tuījiàn	v.	recommend	S	9A
180	外面	wàimiàn	n.	outside	G	2A
181	晚餐	wǎncān	n.	supper	G	1A
182	万	wàn	num.	ten thousand	G	9A
183	万谷湖	Wàngǔ Hú	pn.	Boeung Kak Lake	G	9A
184	忘	wàng	v.	forget	G	8B
185	为什么	wèi shénme	phr.	why	G	6B
186	位	wèi	m.	*a measure word used in deferential reference to people*	G	2A
187	无线	wúxiàn	adj.	wireless	S	6A
188	吴哥窟	Wúgēkū	pn.	Angkor Wat	G	9A
189	午餐	wǔcān	n.	lunch	G	1A

（续表）

序号	生词	拼音	词性	词义	普通G/专业S	所属单元
190	物品	wùpǐn	n.	goods	G	5B
191	西餐厅	xīcāntīng	phr.	Western restaurant	S	1A
192	洗衣费	xǐyīfèi	phr.	laundry charge	S	10B
193	喜欢	xǐhuan	v.	like	G	1A
194	下车	xià chē	phr.	get off	S	9B
195	现金	xiànjīn	n.	cash	G	4A
196	相当	xiāngdāng	v.	match, correspond to	G	9A
197	相当于	xiāngdāng yú	phr.	be equal to	G	9A
198	小	xiǎo	adj.	small	G	9B
199	效劳	xiào//láo	v.	work for	G	7A
200	协议	xiéyì	n.	agreement	S	10B
201	辛苦	xīnkǔ	adj./v.	hard; work laboriously	G	7B
202	新街口	Xīnjiēkǒu	pn.	Xinjiekou	G	9B
203	星期	xīngqī	n.	week	G	2A
204	星期五	xīngqīwǔ	n.	Friday	G	2A
205	行李箱	xínglixiāng	n.	suitcase	S	5B
206	行李员	xínglǐyuán	n.	porter	S	5A
207	型号	xínghào	n.	model, type	G	8A
208	续住	xù zhù	phr.	extended stay	S	4A
209	选购	xuǎngòu	v.	pick out and buy	S	9B
210	选择	xuǎnzé	v./n.	choose; choice	G	7A
211	押金	yājīn	n.	deposit	S	4A
212	盐水鸭	yánshuǐyā	pn.	salted duck	G	9B
213	一共	yígòng	adv.	altogether	G	10A
214	一日游	yí rì yóu	phr.	one-day tour	S	9A
215	以前	yǐqián	n.	previous time	G	5B
216	一起	yìqǐ	adv./n.	together; being in the same place	G	7B
217	一些	yìxiē	q.	some	G	9A
218	应该	yīnggāi	v.	ought to	G	6A
219	营业	yíngyè	v.	be open	S	1A
220	用	yòng	v.	use	G	6A
221	用户	yònghù	n.	user	G	10B

(续表)

序号	生词	拼音	词性	词义	普通 G/专业 S	所属单元
222	由	yóu	prep.	by	G	2B
223	游泳	yóuyǒng	v./n.	swim	G	1B
224	游泳池	yóuyǒngchí	n.	swimming pool	S	1B
225	有名	yǒu//míng	adj.	famous	G	9A
226	右	yòu	n.	right	G	6A
227	右边	yòubian	n.	right side	G	6A
228	余额	yú'é	n.	balance, remaining sum	G	4A
229	雨花茶	yǔhuāchá	pn.	Yuhua Tea	G	9B
230	预付	yùfù	v.	prepay	S	4A
231	元	yuán	m.	*yuan* (the basic unit of money in China)	G	4A
232	员工	yuángōng	n.	staff	G	3A
233	原因	yuányīn	n.	reason	G	3B
234	远	yuǎn	adj.	far	G	9A
235	云锦	Yúnjǐn	pn.	brocade	G	9B
236	允许	yǔnxǔ	v.	allow	G	6B
237	再	zài	adv.	again	G	6B
238	早餐券	zǎocānquàn	n.	breakfast voucher	S	2A
239	站	zhàn	n.	stop, station	G	9B
240	这些	zhèxiē	pron.	these	G	9B
241	直行	zhí xíng	phr.	go straight	S	9A
242	值得	zhí//dé	v.	be worth	G	9A
243	中餐厅	zhōngcāntīng	phr.	Chinese restaurant	S	1A
244	中国	Zhōngguó	pn.	China	S	2A
245	中心	zhōngxīn	n.	center	G	8B
246	中央	zhōngyāng	n.	center	G	9B
247	种	zhǒng	m.	kind, type	G	7A
248	转	zhuǎn	v.	turn	G	9A
249	转接头	zhuǎnjiētóu	n.	adapter	S	8B
250	转账	zhuǎn//zhàng	v.	transfer accounts	S	2B
251	准备	zhǔnbèi	v.	prepare	G	2B
252	资料	zīliào	n.	information, data	G	2A
253	自己	zìjǐ	pron.	oneself	G	7B

137

（续表）

序号	生词	拼音	词性	词义	普通G/专业S	所属单元
254	租借	zūjiè	v.	rent	S	8A
255	租借物品单	zūjiè wùpǐndān	phr.	rental list	S	8A
256	左	zuǒ	n.	left	G	9A
257	左右	zuǒyòu	n.	used in a numeral to indicate approximation	G	5B

日常用语
Daily Expressions

1. 我们有一个中餐厅和一个西餐厅。
2. 早餐从早上 6:00 到 10:00，午餐从中午 11:30 到下午 2:00，晚餐从下午 6:00 开始，9:30 结束。
3. 祝您用餐愉快！
4. 洗衣房是免费使用的。
5. 会议室在三楼。
6. 您可以使用房间内提供的保险箱。
7. 您能告诉我你们团队的名字吗？
8. 我查到了你们的预订记录，10 个双人间，今晚入住。
9. 请登记一下团队的资料。
10. 这是你们的房卡和早餐券。
11. 我可以看看你们的护照吗？
12. 我可以确认你们的离店时间吗？
13. 请问你们要怎么付款呢？
14. 请您在这里签上名字和电话号码。
15. 这是你们的证件，请收好。
16. 请填写团队资料登记表。
17. 请问您想换什么房间？
18. 行李员会把行李送到你们的房间。
19. 请问是什么原因？
20. 请稍等，我查一下空房的情况。
21. 客房的员工会来帮您拿行李。
22. 请您在房间等候。
23. 我可以帮您换成园景房。
24. 园景房在城景房的反方向，面对酒店的花园。
25. 请问您还要续住几天？
26. 请问您是付现金还是刷信用卡？
27. 请您预付 500 元。
28. 这是您的房卡和押金收据，请收好。
29. 麻烦您一会儿到前台办理续住申请。
30. 请领取您的新房卡。
31. 如果您愿意搬到其他楼层的房间，我们可以为您安排。
32. 我查一下后两天的客房住宿情况。
33. 需要我为您联系别的酒店吗？
34. 现在是旅游旺季，酒店没有空余房间，很抱歉！
35. 感谢您的续住，祝您愉快！
36. 抱歉，您的房间明天已经被预订了。
37. 您介意换一个房间吗？
38. 麻烦您填写行李牌。
39. 随后我们会安排行李员将您的行李送到您的房间。

40. 是现在送行李还是其他时间呢?
41. 请问您要寄存几件行李?
42. 请问您的行李箱中有贵重物品吗?
43. 请问您什么时候来取?
44. 请在晚上 9:00 以前来取行李。
45. 可以借用您的房卡刷电梯吗?
46. 这是您的两个行李箱吗?
47. 请交还行李牌。
48. 如果您有任何疑问,可以联系我们。
49. 您能在您的电脑上找到网络图标吗?
50. 网络图标通常在任务栏的右边。
51. 请点击网络图标,看可用网络列表。
52. 您应该能看到我们酒店的网络名称。
53. 现在点击连接按钮,密码是房间号码。
54. 酒店里所有地方都有免费无线网。
55. 没有密码。
56. 您只需要使用您的房间号来登录。
57. 我能更改一下您手机的设置吗?
58. 已经改好了,您再试一下。
59. 我们有两种套餐供您选择,牛肉面套餐和鸡肉饭套餐。您喜欢哪种?
60. 您想喝什么,茶、咖啡还是红酒?
61. 跟您确认一下,一份牛肉面套餐,一壶绿茶。
62. 马上为您准备,送餐员会按时送到。
63. 这是您点的餐,给您放在这里可以吗?
64. 绿茶需要现在给您倒上吗?
65. 您是想付现金还是挂账?
66. 请把您的姓名和房号签在账单上。
67. 祝您用餐愉快!
68. 请问您是几位用餐?
69. 这是您预订的午餐。
70. 您希望几点送餐?
71. 需要为您提供租借服务吗?
72. 请提供一下您需要充电的手机型号。
73. 麻烦您在这边的租借物品单上登记一下。
74. 如果您有任何需要,请随时联系我们。
75. 请问您的姓名和房间号?
76. 需要为您送到房间吗?
77. 住店客人免费租借。
78. 稍后客房服务员会把转接头给您送去。
79. 请问您需要租借什么物品?
80. 我马上安排客房服务人员给您送过去。
81. 您可以送到前台,也可以联系客房中心,工作人员会到房间取走。

82. 不需要押金，只要出示您的身份证件或房卡。
83. 大约20公里，您可以乘坐出租车，半小时就到了。
84. 3万瑞尔，大约相当于50元人民币。
85. 您可以在酒店报名一日游。
86. 您出酒店后左转，直行到第二个红绿灯路口再右转。
87. 在您右边就有一家大超市。
88. 您可以在酒店门口乘坐地铁1号线在新街口站下车，或者3路公交车在新街口东站下车。
89. 您可以去逛一逛新街口百货公司、中央商场。
90. 您可以尝尝雨花茶、盐水鸭。
91. 您也可以选购一些云锦小饰物，这些在市中心的商场都可以买到。
92. 不远，坐出租车的话大概20分钟能到。
93. 今天去的话时间有点儿赶，您可以明天去。
94. 博物馆入口处可以安排导游服务，提供中文、英语、法语和日语讲解服务。
95. 我来打印账单明细给您。
96. 您一共需要付880美元，请您核对。
97. 对了，1516房间的电话费还没有结清。
98. 请您在账单上签字。请问您怎么支付？
99. 这是您的发票。期待您的再次光临。
100. 你们一共五间会议用房，都是您来结账，对吗？
101. 贵公司是我们的挂账协议用户，您有权限挂单结账。
102. 这是您的账单。没有问题的话，请签字。
103. 这是您的挂账单和账单明细，请收好。
104. 房卡都收齐了吗？
105. 你们是6月3号入住的，共五间标准间，对吗？
106. 每间房价格是500元一晚，两晚共5000元。
107. 608房间有一笔电话费80元，609房间有一笔SPA的费用368元，麻烦您通知客人结清。

视频脚本
Video Scripts

第一单元　酒店设施介绍

一、热身

A. 您好！这是酒店的中餐厅，营业时间是早上 7:00 到 11:00。
B. 您好！这是酒店的大堂吧，营业时间是晚上 8:00 到 12:00。
C. 您好！这是酒店的西餐厅，营业时间是中午 11:00 到下午 2:00。
D. 您好！这是酒店的会议室，可在早上 8:00 到晚上 9:00 使用。

二、课文 A

客人：打扰一下，餐厅在哪里？
前台接待员：您好，我们有一个中餐厅和一个西餐厅，您喜欢哪一个？
客人：我想尝尝中餐厅的食物。
前台接待员：中餐厅在 2 楼。
客人：餐厅什么时间营业？
前台接待员：早餐在早上 6:00 到 10:00，午餐在早上 11:30 到下午 2:00，晚餐在下午 6:00 开始，9:30 结束。
客人：好的，谢谢。现在几点？
前台接待员：现在是下午 6:30。
客人：那我可以去餐厅用餐了。
前台接待员：是的，祝您用餐愉快！

课文 B

前台接待员：您好，请问有什么可以帮到您。
客人：您好，请问会议室在哪里？
前台接待员：会议室在三楼。
客人：好的，请问健身房在哪里？
前台接待员：健身房在五楼。
客人：可以游泳吗？
前台接待员：酒店的游泳池在四楼。
客人：请问晚餐几点结束？
前台接待员：西餐厅营业到晚上 10:00，中餐厅营业到晚上 9:00。
客人：好的，谢谢。

三、视听说

前台接待员：您好，这是您客人们的房卡。
旅行团领队：好的，谢谢。
前台接待员：入住前我向您介绍一下酒店的设施以及营业时间。
旅行团领队：好的。
前台接待员：早餐餐厅在酒店的一楼，早餐时间为早上 8:00 到 10:00。酒店会议室在二楼，健身房在三楼。
旅行团领队：好的，请问酒店有西餐厅吗？
前台接待员：有的，西餐厅在顶楼，可以看到城市景观。

旅行团领队：好的，谢谢。前台能保管贵重物品吗？
前台接待员：您可以使用房间内提供的保险箱。
旅行团领队：好的，知道了，谢谢。
前台接待员：不客气，祝您入住愉快！

四、学以致用

顾客：请问酒店洗衣房在哪里？
服务员：酒店洗衣房在五楼！
顾客：洗衣房是免费使用的吗？
服务员：是的，洗衣房是免费使用的。
顾客：非常感谢。
服务员：不客气！

第二单元　团队入住登记

一、热身

前台：您好，有什么可以帮您？
客人：我们团队在你们酒店预订了七间房，我是这个团队的领队王芳。
前台：我查到了你们的预订记录，十个双人间，今晚入住，对吗？
客人：是的。麻烦帮我办理入住。
前台：请出示您的护照。
客人：好的，我们这边有统一的团队签证。
前台：请登记一下团队的资料。
客人：好的，我登记好了。
前台：这是你们的房卡和早餐券。早餐营业时间是 6:00，餐厅在三楼。

二、课文 A

客人：下午好，我想为我们团队办理入住。柬埔寨国际旅行社帮我们预订了八个房间。
前台接待员：好的，先生。您能告诉我你们团队的名字吗？
客人：中国旅行团。
前台接待员：好的，你是领队吗？怎么称呼您？
客人：是的，我叫李宁。
前台接待员：李先生，我们已经查到你们团队的预订资料了。您的团队共有十位男士和六位女士，预订了八间双人间，其中有四对夫妇，对吗？团队成员现在都还在外面吗？
客人：是的。他们还在巴士车上。
前台接待员：你们将在星期五退房，有什么变化吗？
客人：没有。
前台接待员：好的，李先生。我可以看看你们的签证吗？
客人：可以。
前台接待员：请填写团队资料登记表。你们的房间在第 12 层，这是带早餐券的房卡。
客人：谢谢，你能为我们安排早上 7:00 的叫醒电话吗？
前台接待员：没问题，行李员会把行李送到你们的房间。祝你们住得愉快。

课文 B

客人：你好！我们团队在你们酒店预订了七间房，我是这个团队的领队王芳。
前台接待员：请稍等，我查一下我们的预订记录。你们团 14 个人，预订的是 6 月 2 日、3 日两晚的七间海景房，是吗？

客人：是的，麻烦帮我办理入住。
前台接待员：当然可以，女士，我们已经准备好了登记表，麻烦出示以下你们团队14人的护照。
客人：好的，我们这边有统一的团队签证。
前台接待员：好的，我可以确认你们的离店时间吗？
客人：我们6月4日早上9:00退房。
前台接待员：好的，请问你们要怎么付款呢？
客人：所有费用都由我们旅行社转账支付给你们酒店。
前台接待员：好的，你们的房间在同一层。这是你们的房卡和早餐券，请分给你的成员，请您在这里签上名字和电话号码，好吗？
客人：好的。
前台接待员：这是你们的证件，请收好。希望您在这里住得愉快！
客人：好的，谢谢。

三、视听说

前台：早上好，请问谁是领队？
领队：我。
前台：您好，我是莉莉。欢迎入住我们酒店，我想确认一下您的入住安排计划表。
领队：好的。
前台：请问入住人数有变化吗？需要入住的房间类型有变化吗？
领队：没有。
前台：好的，您的退房时间是明天上午9:00，对吗？
领队：我们要改到9:30。
前台：那原来安排的早上7:00叫早服务需要更改到7:30吗？
领队：好的。
前台：请问您能让团队成员在明天早上9:00前将行李放在房间门口吗？行李员会来取。是否还需要其他服务呢？
领队：没有了，就这些，谢谢。
前台：谢谢，希望您在这儿过得愉快！

四、学以致用

前台：您好，欢迎入住我们酒店，我想确认一下您的入住安排计划表。
领队：好的。
前台：请问入住人数有变化吗？需要入住的房间类型有变化吗？
领队：没有。16人，四间双人房，两间单人房，一间三人房，一间行政套房。
前台：好的，您的退房时间是7月19日下午2:00，对吗？
领队：我们要改到早上9:30。
前台：那原来安排的早上7:00叫早服务需要更改到7:30吗？
领队：好的。
前台：请问您能让团队成员在明天早上9:00前将行李放在房间门口吗？行李员会来取。是否还需要其他服务呢？
领队：早餐几点？
前台：早餐在二楼中餐厅，9:30之前都可以用餐。请问你们要怎么付款呢？
领队：所有费用都由我们旅行社转账支付给你们酒店。

第三单元　调换房间

一、热身

客人：你好，我想换房间。

前台：能告诉我是什么原因吗？

客人：太吵了。

前台：我先查询一下房态情况。你好，酒店现在还有空房，可以为您调换。

客人：谢谢！

二、课文 A

前台接待员：您好，请问有什么可以帮到您？

客人：您好，我是303房间的客人，我想调换一下房间。

前台接待员：好的，303是大床房，请问您想换什么房间？

客人：明天有客户来访问，我想换一间套房。

前台接待员：好的，套房在六楼。

客人：请问套房有会客厅吗？

前台接待员：是的，套房有一间会客厅。

客人：好的，请帮我调换。

前台接待员：客房的员工会来帮您拿行李。

客人：好的，谢谢。

前台接待员：不客气，请您在房间等候。

课文 B

客人：你好，我想调换一下房间。

前台接待员：您好，请问是什么原因？

客人：我的房间对着马路，有点儿吵。

前台接待员：好的，您预订的是城景房，我可以帮您换成园景房。

客人：园景房在什么方向。

前台接待员：园景房在城景房的反方向，面对酒店的花园。

客人：好的，谢谢。

前台接待员：不客气！

三、视听说

旅行团领队：你好！我是南方旅行团的领队，我想帮我的客人调换一下房间。

前台接待员：请问您客人的名字是？

旅行团领队：李林。

前台接待员：请问您客人的房间号？

旅行团领队：房间号是303。

前台接待员：您的客人已经预订了一间双床房，请问要换成什么房型？

旅行团领队：换成大床房。

前台接待员：好的，我帮您调换，这是您的新房卡。

旅行团领队：谢谢！

四、学以致用

我们学习了酒店各种房间类型，现在假设你是光明旅行团的领队，酒店前台将一号家庭分在了B房间，二号家庭分在了C房间，三号家庭分在了A房间。你发现这样不合适，请为他们调换房间。

第四单元　续住服务

一、热身

客人：你好，我想要办理续住。

前台：你好，我先查看一下房态情况。有空房，可以续住，请您再次预付押金。

客人：好的。

前台：这是您的新房卡，请收好！

客人：谢谢！

二、课文 A

客人：你好，我想办理续住。

前台接待员：好的，请问您的姓名和房号？

客人：王仪，房号是 1305。

前台接待员：请问您还要续住几天？

客人：两天。

前台接待员：请问您是付现金还是刷信用卡？

客人：现金。

前台接待员：请您预付 500 元，谢谢。

前台接待员：这是您的房卡和押金收据，请收好，感谢您的续住，祝您愉快！

客人：谢谢！

课文 B

客人：你好，我想要办理续住。

前台接待员：请问您的房间号是多少？

客人：601。我本来打算今天退房的，但现在我想多住一天。

前台接待员：请稍等。

客人：好的。

前台接待员：不好意思，先生。您的房间明天已经被预订了。您介意换一个房间吗？

客人：可以。

前台接待员：感谢您的理解。麻烦您一会儿到前台来办理续住申请并领取您的新卡。

三、视听说

客人：你好，我想办理续住。

前台接待员：先生，请问您的姓名和房号？

客人：李明，1505 房间。

前台接待员：请问您想再住多久？

客人：我想再住两天。

前台接待员：请稍等，我查一下后两天的客房住宿情况。

客人：好的，谢谢。

前台接待员：先生，让您久等了，我们明天将有两个旅行团到达，他们预订了 15 层的所有房间。

客人：那怎么办呢？

前台接待员：如果您愿意搬到其他楼层的房间，我们可以为您安排。

客人：那太好了，谢谢你。

第五单元　行李服务

一、热身

A 填写行李牌

前台：我们有行李员帮您拿行李到房间，请填写行李牌。

客人：填写好了，给你。

行李员：您好，请问这是您的三件行李吗？

　　客人：是的。

行李员：您的房间号是多少？

　　客人：506。

B 行李员把行李交给客人

行李员：请问还有别的需要帮忙吗？

　　客人：暂时没有，谢谢！

C 客人询问前台关于行李服务

　　客人：因为我的行李比较多，可以帮我把行李拿到房间吗？

　　前台：可以的。

D 客人办理入住

　　客人：你好，办理入住。

　　前台：欢迎光临，请问你的姓名和电话？

　　客人：李晓明，13900000000。

二、课文 A

　　客人：你好，可以将我的行李送到我的房间吗？

礼宾员：好的，是现在送还是其他时间呢？

　　客人：过半个小时后．

礼宾员：好的，麻烦您填写行李牌。

　　客人：好的。

礼宾员：随后我们会安排行李员将您的行李送到您的房间。

　　客人：谢谢。

课文 B

　　　　客人：你好，我想寄存行李。

前台接待员：请问您要寄存几件行李？

　　　　客人：两个行李箱。

前台接待员：请问您的行李箱中有贵重物品吗？

　　　　客人：没有。

前台接待员：请问您的姓名和房间号？

　　　　客人：王仪，1606。

前台接待员：请问您什么时候来取？

　　　　客人：今天下午 5:00 左右。

前台接待员：1606 号房间王女士寄存行李箱两个，没有贵重物品。请在晚上 9:00 以前来取行李。

　　　　客人：好的，谢谢！

前台接待员：不客气！

三、视听说

礼宾员：下午好，先生。我将带您去房间，这是您的两个行李箱吗？

　　客人：是的。

礼宾员：请问您的行李里有贵重物品或易碎物品吗？

　　客人：没有。

礼宾员：这边请。

礼宾员：先生，可以借用您的房卡刷电梯吗？

客人：给你。
礼宾员：您的房间到了，您先请，我可以把您的行李放在这里吗？
客人：可以。
礼宾员：请问还有什么可以帮您吗？
客人：没有了，就这些。
礼宾员：如果您有任何疑问，可以联系我们。
客人：好的，谢谢你！

四、学以致用

行李员敲门并表明自己身份；客人打开房门；客人核对行李，并表示感谢；行李员拿回行李牌；祝愿客人入住愉快。

第六单元　网络服务

一、热身

A 询问前台如何连接酒店无线网络

客人：你好，请问如何我的手机如何能连接酒店的无线网络？

B 询问前台网络密码

客人：请问酒店无线网络的密码是多少？

C 房间网络不稳定，电话咨询前台

客人：你好，我刚刚连接酒店的无线网络，显示网络不稳定，请问这是怎么回事？

D 请工作人员帮助连无线网络

客人：请问你能帮我把手机连接上酒店的无线网络吗？

二、课文 A

客人：你好，我想知道在我的房间能不能接入无线网络？
前台服务员：可以的。
客人：能告诉我怎么连接笔记本电脑吗？
前台服务员：您能在您的电脑上找到网络图标吗？它通常在任务栏的右边。
客人：好的。
前台服务员：现在请点击网络图标看可用网络列表，您应该能看到我们酒店的无线网络名称。
客人：好的，我看到了。
前台服务员：现在点击按钮连接，密码是房间号码。
客人：太棒了，我能上网了。
前台服务员：请问还有什么需要帮忙吗？
客人：不用了，谢谢。

课文 B

客人：你好，我想知道酒店里面有没有无线网络？
前台接待员：有的，酒店所有地方都有免费无线网，没有密码，您只需要使用您的名字和房间号来登录。
客人：好的，我试一下。不知道为什么我的手机上不了网。
前台接待员：我能看一下您的手机吗？
客人：当然。
前台接待员：我能更改一下您手机的设置吗？
客人：为什么？
前台接待员：您的手机设置了不允许连接公共无线网。

客人：好的。
前台接待员：已经改好了，您再试一下。
客人：可以了，谢谢。

三、视听说
客人：你好，我是1606房间的客人，我的手机没办法连接酒店的无线网络。请问是什么原因呢？
前台接待员：无线网络名称是金陵酒店，密码是您的房间号1606。
客人：我再试一次，现在连接上了。
前台接待员：好的，请问还有什么需要帮助吗？
客人：没有了，谢谢！
前台接待员：不客气，祝您入住愉快！

四、学以致用
打开手机，找到设置，选择无线局域网，寻找酒店名称，输入密码，点击连接，连接成功。

第七单元　房内用餐服务

一、热身
A. 总机员：你好！这是总机，请问有什么能为您效劳？
B. 客房服务员：你好！客房服务。
　　客人：您好，麻烦给207房间送一床被子。
C. 服务员：您好，欢迎光临。请问您是几位用餐？
D. 送餐员：您好，送餐员！这是您预订的午餐，给您放在这里可以吗？

二、课文 A
总机员：上午好，请问有什么能为您效劳？
客人：您好，我想在房间用午餐，需要送餐服务。
总机员：我们有两种套餐供您选择，牛肉面套餐和鸡肉饭套餐。您喜欢哪种？
客人：我想点牛肉面套餐。
总机员：您想喝什么，茶、咖啡还是红酒？
客人：来一壶绿茶。
总机员：跟您确认一下，一份牛肉面套餐，一壶绿茶。
客人：抱歉，我们是两人用餐，两份牛肉面，一壶绿茶。请中午11:30送餐。
总机员：好的，马上为您准备，送餐员会按时送到。
客人：谢谢。

课文 B
送餐员：您好，送餐员。
客人：您好，请进。
送餐员：这是您点的餐，给您放在这里可以吗？
客人：没有问题，辛苦你了。
送餐员：绿茶需要给您现在倒上吗？
客人：我自己来就可以了。
送餐员：您是想付现金还是挂账？
客人：挂账吧，退房的时候我一起结账。
送餐员：好的，请把您的姓名和房号签在账单上。谢谢，祝您用餐愉快！

三、视听说

总机员：您好，这里是总机，有什么可以帮您？
客　人：请问酒店今天有什么午餐供应？我想在房内用餐。
总机员：今天中午有牛排套餐和意面套餐供您选择。
客　人：给我来一份意面套餐吧。
总机员：跟您确认一下，您点了意面套餐，一人食用。您希望几点送餐？
客　人：12:00 吧。
总机员：好的，已经为你登记，送餐员会准时为您送到房间。
客　人：谢谢。

四、学以致用

您好，我是 311 房间的陆先生，我想点一份鸡肉饭套餐和一杯绿茶，麻烦 11:30 送到我的房间，谢谢。

您好，今天中午我想在房间用餐，麻烦 12:30 帮我送一份牛肉面套餐和一杯咖啡，咖啡加奶不加糖。对了，我是 520 房间的李小姐。

前台吗？我是 1014 房间的余小姐。我想 7:00 在房间用晚餐，能帮我点两份牛排套餐和两杯红酒吗？

第八单元　租借服务

一、热身

一般来说，酒店都会提供相应的租借服务，这些物品包含：雨伞、充电器、烧水壶、电吹风、电熨斗等。如果你需要使用，可以到前台进行租借登记，办理租借手续。

二、课文 A

客　　　人：您好！我是 801 房间的李明。我的手机没电了。
前台接待员：需要为您提供租借服务吗？
客　　　人：是的，请问你们这里有手机充电器吗？
前台接待员：请提供一下您需要充电的手机型号。
客　　　人：华为 Mate 9。
前台接待员：好的，麻烦您在这边的租借物品单上登记一下。
客　　　人：登记好了，用完之后我就归还回来。
前台接待员：没问题，如果您有任何需要，请随时联系我们。
客　　　人：谢谢！

课文 B

客房中心：这里是客房服务中心，有什么可以帮到您？
客　　人：您好，我忘带转接头了，酒店提供租借服务吗？
客房中心：提供的，请问您的姓名和房间号。
客　　人：李华，我的房间号是 508。
客房中心：请稍等，我登记一下，需要为您送到房间吗？
客　　人：好的，这是免费服务么？
客房中心：是的，住店客人免费租借。稍后客房服务员会把转接头给您送过去。
客　　人：谢谢！

三、视听说

总机接线员：您好，这里是总机，有什么可以帮到您？
客　　　人：酒店提供租借服务吗？

总机接线员：请问您需要租借什么用品？
  客人：我需要熨一下衣服，有没有电熨斗可供租借？
总机接线员：有的，麻烦您提供一下房号和姓名，我登记一下。
  客人：我姓王，我住207房间。
总机接线员：好的，我记下来了。我马上安排客房服务人员给您送过去。
  客人：用完之后，我怎么归还？
总机接线员：您可以送到前台，也可以联系客房中心，工作人员会到房间取走。

四、学以致用

客人：你好！请问酒店有雨伞吗？
前台：你好！有的。
客人：我可以借用一天吗？
前台：当然可以。
客人：需要押金吗？
前台：不需要的，只需要出示您的身份证件或房卡。
客人：好的，谢谢。
前台：不客气！

第九单元　城市及旅游信息服务

一、热身

  王红走出机场，买了张地图，然后乘坐出租车前往一个美丽的景区，在景区入口买了门票，离开景区后她乘坐公交车到达了一个博物馆。

二、课文A

  客人：请问吴哥窟距离酒店多远，怎么去比较方便？
前台接待员：大约20公里，您可以乘坐出租车，半小时就到了。
  客人：出租车费大概要多少元？
前台接待员：30 000瑞尔，大约相当于50元人民币。
  客人：好的，谢谢！柬埔寨还有哪些景区值得去，您能推荐一下吗？
前台接待员：皇宫、塔山寺、万谷湖、巴肯山都很有名，您可以在酒店报名一日游。
  客人：我还想买一些东西，附近有超市吗？
前台接待员：您出酒店后左转，直行到第二个红绿灯路口再右转，在您右边就有一家大超市。
  客人：好的，非常感谢。

课文B

  客人：您好，我想到市中心，怎么去比较方便？
前台接待员：您可以在酒店门口乘坐地铁1号线，或者3路公交车，在新街口站下车。
  客人：好的，新街口有什么大的商场吗？
前台接待员：您可以去逛一逛新街口百货公司、中央商场。
  客人：好的，我想买一些特产，您有什么推荐的吗？
前台接待员：您可以尝尝雨花茶、盐水鸭；另外，您也可以选购一些云锦小饰物。这些在市中心的商场都可以买到。
  客人：好的，谢谢！

三、视听说

前台接待员：下午好！女士，请问您需要我做什么吗？

151

客人：我想带儿子去参观国家博物馆，请问距离酒店远吗？
前台接待员：不远，坐出租车的话大概20分钟能到。您计划什么时候去？
客人：现在去来得及吗？
前台接待员：现在是下午3:00，4:30博物馆会停止售票，5:00关门。今天去的话时间有点儿赶，您可以明天去。
客人：好的，谢谢。请问博物馆有讲解服务吗？
前台接待员：博物馆入口处可以安排导游服务，提供中文、英语、法语和日语讲解服务。

四、学以致用
①地铁站就在我们酒店斜对面，您出门左拐，在路口过个马路就到了。
②从酒店出门右拐，在第一个路口继续右拐，然后直走，邮局在您的右手边。
③从酒店出门右拐，然后在第一个路口左拐，然后直走，很快就能够看到医院在您的正前方。

第十单元　团队退房服务

一、热身
某酒店与旅行社签订了《酒店挂账协议》，该旅行社的导游带旅游团到这个酒店住宿，离店结账时不需要当场支付，而是签字确认账单即可。一个月后，旅行社统一支付团队在该酒店的所有账单。

二、课文A
旅行团领队：您好，我是陈丽，中国国际旅行社的领队。我想给我的团队退房。
前台接待员：好的，请告诉我您的房间号。
旅行团领队：1515到1518，共四间房，从5月8号起入住的。这些是房卡。
前台接待员：好的，请稍等。我来打印账单明细给您。您一共需要付880美元，请您核对。对了，1516房间的电话费还没有结清。
旅行团领队：电话费客人自己付。他可能忘了，我来告诉他。
前台接待员：谢谢，陈女士，请您在账单上签字。请问您怎么支付？
旅行团领队：信用卡支付。
前台接待员：谢谢，这是您的发票。期待您的再次光临。

课文B
客人：你好，我是参加"中国—柬埔寨友好合作会议"的负责人张山，我来给参会的客人办理退房。
前台接待员：张先生，你们一共五间会议用房，都是您来结账，对吗？
客人：是的，房卡给您。
前台接待员：贵公司是我们的挂账协议用户，您有权限挂单结账，请给我您的护照。
客人：802房间的酒水费和805房间的洗衣费由客人自己支付，我会通知他们。
前台接待员：这是您的账单。没有问题的话，请签字。
客人：好的，给您。
前台接待员：好的，这是您的挂账单和账单明细，请收好。
客人：谢谢。

三、视听说
前台接待员：先生，中午好！我能为您做什么？
客人：我是中国旅行社的领队王刚，我要退房。
前台接待员：好的，王先生，房卡都收齐了吗？
客人：收齐了，给您。
前台接待员：你们是6月3号入住的，共五间标准间，对吗？
客人：是的，我们一共住了两晚。

前台接待员：每间房价格是 500 元一晚，两晚共 5000 元。另外，608 房间有一笔电话费 80 元，609 房间有一笔 SPA 的费用 368 元，麻烦您通知客人结清。这是您的账单，请确认。

客人：好的，账单没有问题，我来通知 608 和 609 房间的客人。

前台接待员：好的，谢谢。

四、学以致用

2020 年 5 月，西门子公司在某酒店举办了庆祝公司成立 30 周年的会议，会议时间是 5 月 1 日至 4 日，会议负责人是王军，有签字确认账单挂账的权限。他预订了一间豪华套房、二个大床房和五个标准间，价格分别是 980 元、480 元和 380 元。

参考答案 Reference Answers

第一单元

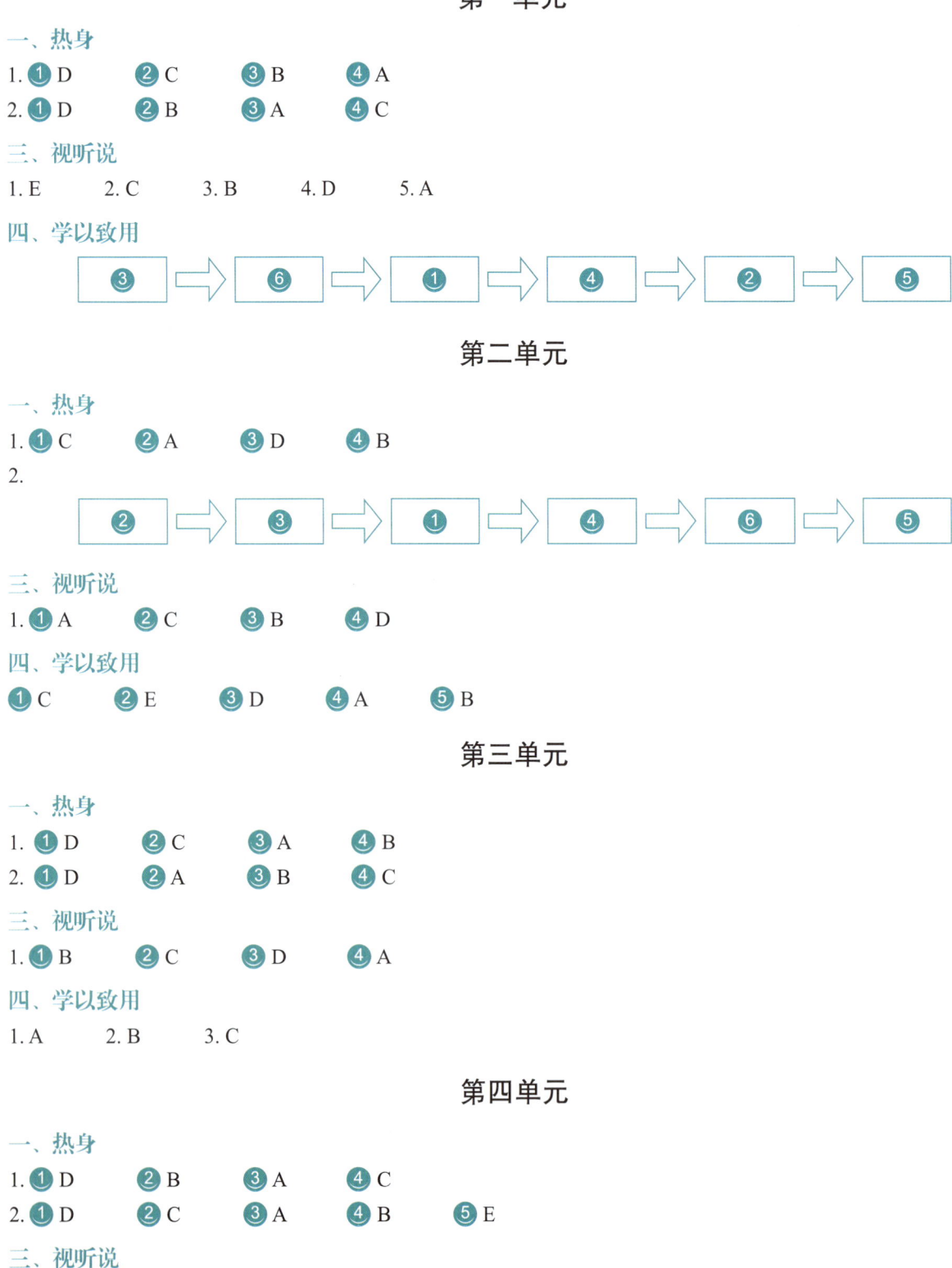

一、热身

1. ① D ② C ③ B ④ A
2. ① D ② B ③ A ④ C

三、视听说

1. E 2. C 3. B 4. D 5. A

四、学以致用

③ → ⑥ → ① → ④ → ② → ⑤

第二单元

一、热身

1. ① C ② A ③ D ④ B
2.

② → ③ → ① → ④ → ⑥ → ⑤

三、视听说

1. ① A ② C ③ B ④ D

四、学以致用

① C ② E ③ D ④ A ⑤ B

第三单元

一、热身

1. ① D ② C ③ A ④ B
2. ① D ② A ③ B ④ C

三、视听说

1. ① B ② C ③ D ④ A

四、学以致用

1. A 2. B 3. C

第四单元

一、热身

1. ① D ② B ③ A ④ C
2. ① D ② C ③ A ④ B ⑤ E

三、视听说

① C ② A ③ B ④ D

四、学以致用

② → ④ → ③ → ⑥ → ⑤ → ① → ⑦

第五单元

一、热身

1. ① C　② B　③ D　④ A
2. ① C　② D　③ A　④ B

三、视听说

① B　② C　③ A　④ D

四、学以致用

② → ⑤ → ④ → ③ → ①

第六单元

一、热身

1. ① C　② D　③ B　④ A
2. ① B　② D　③ C　④ A

三、视听说

① D　② A　③ B　④ C

四、学以致用

③ → ④ → ⑦ → ② → ⑤ → ⑥ → ①

第七单元

一、热身

1. ① D　② B　③ A　④ C
2. ① B　② D　③ A　④ C

三、视听说

② → ③ → ⑤ → ⑥ → ① → ④

四、学以致用

房间号码	客人姓名	点餐	数量	备注
311	陆先生	鸡肉饭套餐，绿茶	1	
520	李小姐	牛肉面套餐、咖啡	1	加奶不加糖
1014	余小姐	牛排套餐、红酒	2	

第八单元

一、热身

1. ① D　② C　③ A　④ B

2. ① A ② C ③ B

三、视听说

④ → ③ → ⑤ → ① → ②

四、学以致用

① B ② A ③ D ④ C

第九单元

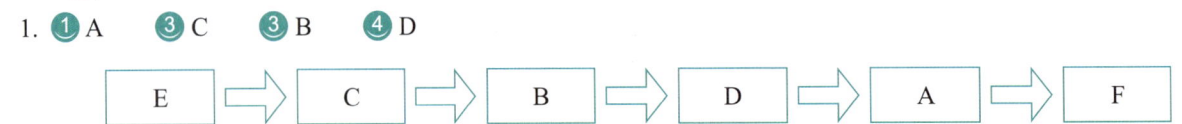

一、热身

1. ① A ② C ③ B ④ D

E → C → B → D → A → F

三、视听说

1. BD 2. EC 3. A

四、学以致用

① A ② BBB ③ BAB

第十单元

一、热身

1. ① C ② A ③ B ④ D

2. B

三、视听说

⑤ → ② → ⑥ → ④ → ① → ③

四、学以致用

酒店客房账单明细					
公司	西门子		国籍	中国	
团队类型	团队		会议√		
抵店日期	2020年5月1日				
离店日期	2020年5月4日				
房间类型	标准间	大床房	豪华套间	合计（元）	
房间数量	5	2	1	3840	
房间单价（元/晚）	380	480	980		
支付方式	现金	信用卡	支票	挂账√	
客人签字	王军（手写）				